T0330587

ROUTLEDGE LIBRARY EDITIONS: EMPLOYEE OWNERSHIP AND ECONOMIC DEMOCRACY

Volume 13

PARTICIPATIVE MANAGEMENT

PARTICIPATIVE MANAGEMENT
An Analysis of its Effect on Productivity

DR MICHAEL H. SWEARINGEN

Routledge
Taylor & Francis Group

LONDON AND NEW YORK

First published in 1997 by Garland Publishing, Inc.

This edition first published in 2018
by Routledge
2 Park Square, Milton Park, Abingdon, Oxon OX14 4RN

and by Routledge
711 Third Avenue, New York, NY 10017

Routledge is an imprint of the Taylor & Francis Group, an informa business

British Library Cataloguing in Publication Data
A catalogue record for this book is available from the British Library

ISBN: 978-1-138-29962-7 (Set)
ISBN: 978-1-315-12163-5 (Set) (ebk)
ISBN: 978-1-138-56099-4 (Volume 13) (hbk)
ISBN: 978-0-203-71112-5 (Volume 13) (ebk)

Publisher's Note
The publisher has gone to great lengths to ensure the quality of this reprint but points out that some imperfections in the original copies may be apparent.

Disclaimer
The publisher has made every effort to trace copyright holders and would welcome correspondence from those they have been unable to trace.

PARTICIPATIVE MANAGEMENT

AN ANALYSIS OF ITS EFFECT ON PRODUCTIVITY

MICHAEL H. SWEARINGEN

GARLAND PUBLISHING, INC.
NEW YORK & LONDON / 1997

Library of Congress Cataloging-in-Publication Data

Swearingen, Michael H.
    Participative management : an analysis of its effect on
productivity / Michael H. Swearingen.
        p.   cm. — (Garland studies on industrial productivity)
    Revision of thesis (Ed.D.)—Western Michigan University,
1995.
    Includes bibliographical references and index.
    ISBN 0-8153-2825-7 (alk. paper)
    1. Industrial management—Employee participation.
2. Industrial productivity. 3. Organizational change—Management. 4. Organizational effectiveness. 5. Quality of work life.
I. Title. II. Series.
HD5650.S9 1997
331.11'8—dc21

                                                    96-46725

Printed on acid-free, 250-year-life paper
Manufactured in the United States of America

Dedication

Not being a "traditional" student, my path on the road of knowledge has been long and rocky. Frequently, just prior to the completion of a long project, I found myself wondering if I really wanted to continue or just pull the plug and let everything quietly expire. It was during these periods that my wife, through both flattery and threats, helped me jump start myself again. Without her help and patience, I never would have finished.

I would also like to thank Al Demers, Simonds Industries Corporate Manager for Accounts Receivable/Payable. Al performed a lifesaving act by getting me the financial information I needed on the various organizations that responded. Without Al's help, my fifth hypothesis could never have been tested.

Last, but not least, I would like to thank my committee members, Dr. Dale Brethower, Dr. Patrick Jenlink, but most especially Dr. Uldis Smidchens.

I could not have done it without the people mentioned and I want each of them to know how much I appreciate their help and concern.

Contents

List of Tables

ix

Participative Management

I

INTRODUCTION

STATEMENT OF THE PROBLEM

Much has been said about participative management. Its adherents, companies such as Hewlett-Packard, Harman International Industries, Cooperativa Central, International Group Plans, and British Triumph Motorcycle, to name a few, tout it as the cure for all ills while its opponents, including General Foods, McCaysville Industries, Rushton Mining Company, and Vermont Asbestos Group, label it as an ivory tower pipe dream, unworkable in the "real world".

Those who are in favor of a participative style of management state that the persons who oppose it really do not understand what they are opposing, that participative management leads to increased productivity by increasing employee involvement, and this leads to increased employee morale, which helps boost productivity even farther. Participative management is composed of several essential ingredients, including increased communication, quality circles (QC), quality of work life (QWL), joint decision making, conflict resolution, increased job satisfaction, and increased cooperation. There are other parts of the participative management system, but they play a relatively minor role as compared to the listed building blocks (Glaser, 1973).

Some organizations have a written policy stating that they believe in and use a participative management style of management (South Bend Lathe, Inc., Saratoga Knitting Mill, and Mohawk Valley Community Corporation, for example), however, it commonly becomes the case that although the organization may subscribe to or pay lip service to the goal of participative management, the communication is still from the top down with all decision and policy making held in the hands of the top management personnel. This could be caused by several factors, including unfamiliarity with what participative management really is and how it works, and a static organization that has become complacent and actually does not want to "rock the boat". One of the most commonly voiced concerns is how much it will affect productivity and the "bottom line". If a program increases productivity, but costs more than the additional productivity it generates, then the program is essentially useless, since the goal of nearly all organizations, unless they are non-profit or governmental agencies, is to make a profit.

PURPOSE OF THE STUDY

This study examined the relationship between the style of management used and level of productivity, measured in terms of the organization's financial stability. Other variables examined included the age of the top level managers, their educational level, the size and age of the organization, and the organization's physical parameters.

The answers the respondents gave to the Profile of Organizational Characteristics (POC), were grouped for managers within the same organization. The responses from within the organization were averaged to produce a set of single values for each organization that were then compared to other organizations as well as other factors, including financial stability. Chapter II consists of the following major sections devoted to the various aspects of participative management: increased communications, quality circles, quality of work life, joint decision making, conflict resolutions, increased job satisfaction, increased cooperation and productivity.

The information used in designing and and testing the various hypotheses came from many sources, including various periodicals, books, papers presented at professional conferences, studies performed by governmental agencies and educational institutions and dissertations, to name a few.

The following hypotheses were tested:

1. The higher the education level of the organization's managers is, the more likely they are to use a participative management style of management.

2. The older an organization is, the less likely they are to use a participative style of management.

3. The older the organization's managers are, the less likely they are to use a participative style of management.

4. Organizations that use a participative style of management are more likely to be smaller in size than organizations that use a more rigid style of management.

5. Organizations that use a participative style of management will have increased productivity that will result in increased financial stability.

SUMMARY

By determining whether or not productivity is affected by the use of a participative style of management, we are laying the ground work for making companies more competitive. As companies become more competitive, the cost of the items they produce becomes lower, allowing the consumer to spend less money on individual products which, in turn, allows them to make additional purchases of other items. The conclusions from this study could point the way to making companies more competitive by adding additional information to the management process.

II

REVIEW OF RELATED LITERATURE

INTRODUCTION

A great number of studies have dealt with the concept of participative management, what factors enhance it, what factors detract from it and what factors influence whether or not it will even work. A review of the literature was necessary to help determine the factors involved in defining whether or not other studies that were done previously even addressed the issues that were targeted or if they were pertinent, what the results were. The studies reviewed were divided into one of seven categories, increased communication, quality circles (QC), quality of work life (QWL), joint decision making, conflict resolution, increased job satisfaction, increased cooperation and productivity (Glaser, 1973).

A number of sources were used in this review including periodicals, books by established participative management experts, government and educational agency publications, dissertations, article abstracts and other materials.

INCREASED COMMUNICATION

One of the most pressing concerns of a management team trying to start a participative management program is free flowing communicatio between the employees and the managers.

Laura Struebing (1996) reported on a survey of 905 non-management personnel and 611 management personnel that was conducted concerning communication. The report showed the following: 1) 42% of the workers and 51% of the managers felt that they were not valued, 2) only 37% of the workers believed that their supervisor knew what motivates them and worse, only 44% of the supervisors felt that they knew what motivated their employees, 3) less than 46% of workers surveyed felt that their co-workers were happy, but management believed that 67% of the workers were happy working where they were, 4) more than 35% of the organizations who had no formal performance appraisal system and 72% of the managers of surveyed saw no need for one, 5) only 40% of the employees reported that they had received recognition for a good job and only 49% of the managers said that they give it, but 63% of the workers and 58% of the managers say that when they make a mistake, they always hear about it 6) only 59% of the employees think that managers have realistic expectations while 79% of the managers feel expectations are reasonable.

The survey showed that there is a woeful lack of communication between workers and managers, hardly conducive to the establishment of a participative management system.

Theological seminaries, as a rule, are rather bound by tradition, however, Isenhart (1986) examined the issue of increasing employee participation in the decision making and management processes of a Roman Catholic seminary. Data were collected on how the decisions were made after Likert's Profile of Organizational Analysis (POC) was explained to the participants at the seminary. Each decision, after it was made, was rated by the persons involved as to whether it was made using System 1, 2 3, or 4 (exploitive, benevolent, consultative, and participative). The results demonstrated that there was a shift towards the participative style of management, and that communication more easily flowed both up and down through the hierarchy concerning these joint decisions. The paper concluded on the note that there was little likelihood that employee participation in decision making would advance beyond the present level due to the fact that the Vatican had the final authority over the seminary, even though this style appeared to produce more positive attitudes among the lower echelons.

One of the primary identifying components of a participative style of management is the increase in communication from the lower to upper echelons. One hundred three clerical employees and the lowest level of supervisors were part of a study conducted at a comprehensive eastern university (Wheeless, et al, 1982). The questionnaire filled out by the participants measured communication satisfaction with supervisors, supervisory receptivity to information, decision participation level, actual participation versus desired participation difference, and job satisfaction in relation to the supervisor, coworkers, promotions, compensation, and work. The highest correlations within the study were found to be those of communication satisfaction with the supervisors (0.9596) and satisfaction with supervisors (0.9507) in regards to job satisfaction, that is, job satisfaction appeared to be highly correlated with communication satisfaction with supervisors and general satisfaction with supervision. Interestingly enough, the lowest correlation found to exist (0.4275) was satisfaction with the communication with co-workers correlated with job satisfaction. This study was strictly a survey tool and no training in the style of participative management was given prior to the administration of the survey. The main thrust of this study was to show that job satisfaction is greatest when there is open communication between the workers and supervisors, one of the main premises of participative management. One blot on this otherwise rosy picture occurred when the correlation of 0.43 was found between job satisfaction and communication between co-workers. Communication in a true style of participative management occurs not only up and down, but also within levels, something which is obviously lacking to some extent here.

J. N. Feldman (1993) studied participative management in Europe, specifically in union shops and found out that labor agreements in those shops with participative management are reached easier with fewer problems. The secret to this "less than normal" adversarial bargaining is that the supervisory councils are approximately 50% non management employees. Due to the fact that non management employees have access to financial records, the employees tend to be better informed and more likely to accede to management proposals aimed at keeping the company profitable.

Phillips (1977) conducted research into the types of communication patterns used by two television group owners, whom he defined as fully owning more than one United States commercial television station. The station manager and subordinate managers were given Likert's Profile of Organizational Characteristics to help delineate and define what management style was used to generate communication within the organization. The results of the study were that although both of the general managers had similar roles, the philosophy of one organization was more in line with a participative management style which resulted in more open channels of communication between the various levels in the organization.

Neil Barnhard (1980), developed a continuing education course for the beginning or inexperienced supervisor. It was the feeling of Mr. Barnhard and the program development staff, that the most important areas to concentrate on were leadership, communication, conflict resolution, and motivation skills. The article concentrates on the necessity of the supervisor and subordinate working as a team, with open communication and a share in the decision making process, both of which are essential components of participative management.

Flood (1985) wrote a treatise on effective leadership. His primary contention is that unless you have an effective leadership style, you really won't be leading, but will just happen to be at the head of a pack going in a specific direction. Although he describes his favorite style as consultative, his preferred style has a number of participative management factors leavened in. The primary keys to having good workers are communication, involvement in the decision making process, and group involvement.

Snee (1995) stresses that one of the primary tools used in discovering what motivates or "turns on" the employees is an employee survey. He feels that employee surveys fulfill two (2) important functions, they help identify opportunities for improvement and serve as *an effective communication tool* between managers and employees. In order for surveys to work, that is, to achieve the desired results, they must be planned very carefully, using ideas and concepts generated from focus groups and in-depth surveys, to name a few methods. Once the issues have been delineated and the appropriate questions developed to gather the needed information, it becomes necessary to make sure that both the management and the employees are aware of the survey's purpose and have a clear understanding of what is hoped to be accomplished. Another important consideration is sampling frequency, whether to continuously sample small, random groups or do a large "all organization" sampling every 18 to 24 months. Snee gave several reasons why surveys fail, and some of these include critical issues not be addressed, survey objectives are not clearly stated, survey questions are poorly designed, individual responses are not kept confidential, and management does not take action on the results.

Money is a driving factor or reinforcing event, depending on your point of view, for all people. One of the more common trends in American industry is the introduction of gainsharing programs in the plants. Denis Collins (1995), however, relayed the experience of a company who did not adequately define and outline their gainsharing system before implementing it. While the gainsharing system was in place, the company manipulated how the gain was measured, thereby manipulating how much money the employees would realize from the plan. The details of how the plan worked and why changes were made were poorly communicated to the employees, who in turn, started distrusting how the plan was administered. Labor-management relations got worse and finally the plan was abandoned, a prime example of how you should not manage your company.

One of the primary pruposes of communication between workers and management is for the workers to provide feedback to management as well as feedback from management tom workwers. Tuttle and Lester (1993) discussed how students in TQM classes at Wright-Patterson Air Force base in Ohio expressed the concern that their immediate supervisors did not understand and therefore did not implement acceoted TQM practices. In order to help combat this problem, the Supervisor's TQM Behaviors Evaluation Instrument was developed. This instrument is given to various employees by the supervisor. The six (6) questions, with subsections, are Likert scale based, and the employee who receives it fills it out and returns it to a group leader who compiles all of the questionnaires, and constructs a final report for each individual supervisor, discarding the individual responses. This gives the supervisor a starting point to start developing more appropriate communication behavior. The goal of this instrument is to try and foster communication both up and down the hierarchical ladder.

QUALITY CIRCLES (QC)

Most people consider quality circles (QC) and quality of work life programs (QWL) to be synonymous with the concept of participative management, however, while QC and QWL programs are similar, they do have some differences and are a part of participative management systems, not a system in and of themselves. Savage and Romano (1983) articulated what they perceive as the differences in a paper presented at the Annual Meeting of the Eastern Communication Association. They argued that QCs are usually involve employees with similar backgrounds solving technical problems related to the job whereas with QWL programs, the employees come from different levels and are involved in the entire work environment. The QCs in Japan do not focus their programs strictly on developing solutions for technical problems, rather they offer alternative method for dealing with the company. Through the QC program, the average Japanese worker can assist in planning production, receiving additional training, and assist in modifying the work environment to more carefully suit the workers. QC teams in the United States however, are formed to solve only technical problems and are not allowed to roam outside the technical area of interest. This causes the QC to succeed initially, but fail in the long run since the curiosity of the participants eventually diminishes. The QWL offers a concept similar to what the Japanese use as a QC concept, but involves the employee at a greater level than the Japanese QC does. Whichever a company decides to use, either QC or QWL program, they should be part of an integrated package that comprises a participative management system.

One of the major components normally seen in most participative management programs is quality circles. Small (1987) examined participative management in public school systems, specifically,an elementary and middle school in the Baltimore public school system. Using an open ended questionnaire, the teachers in each building were queried as to what they felt were the most pressing problems facing them each day. The quality circle took the resulting answers and tabulated them, and deciding to tackle the problems which were most frequently mentioned. The teachers involved in the circle would brainstorm to come up with possible solutions to each of the problems, come to a general consensus as to which solution would be the most practical, and finally, submit their recommendations to the appropriate authority. It is the contention of the author that participative management can be introduced into organizations and work successfully as long as there are upper level managers who are willing to commit resources to and support quality circles and participative management.

In 1985, J. P. Elvins investigated how quality circles affected communication within the organization. A random sample consisting of 102 quality circle members from five different organizations were given Likert's Profile of Organizational Characteristics and an open ended survey concerning the respondent's personal experiences with quality circles. The results of the study evidenced the fact that the employees in the quality circles felt that quality circles had positive effects on perceived individual influence, communication with superiors, subordinates and peers. The responses given, however, placed the organizations in either a benevolent exploitative or consultative management system.

Central Piedmont Community College decided to institute a quality circle (QC) program in the media production department (Moretz, 1983). The results of the implementation showed that QC programs can be successful, but they also encountered some problems while establishing its worth. Due to the fact that the QC approach started in industry, there were some faculty members that questioned the applicability of QC programs to an educational setting. Another problem arose due to the number of other required meetings already planned for other items, such as curriculum, etc., limiting the amount of available free time for QC meetings. Interestingly enough, the number of advanced degrees proved to be a two edged sword, allowing the participants to quickly grasp the essentials, but also causing problems due to differing philosophies. Other problems included the "end-of-the-term" slowdown, lack of budget flexibility, how to define "productivity" in education, and worst of all, a number of educators were mired in a feeling of helplessness due to previous tries at making changes and therefore exhibited very low confidence in their ability to change things.

Satterwhite (1982) developed a method for effectively managing quality circles in educational settings, including exercises and assessments. The author felt that the necessary components of a successful quality circle were good planning, trained participants, meeting management, group process, and following through on decisions that came from the group.

Many individuals regard quality circles (QC) as a type of organizational interventional strategy to optimize productivity and product quality through employee participation. Hellweg and Freiberg (1984) investigated a number of quality circles to test the viability of the quality circles concept specifically in terms of whether or not they had any effects on the desired organizational outcomes. The authors felt that although the studies that they reviewed showed promise, most of the studies exhibited little empirical evidence of attainment of the predetermined goals. They felt that future studies should be directed towards testing the specific effects of quality circles on the organization and individual.

QUALITY OF WORK LIFE (QWL)

Quality of work life (QWL) is a fairly recent development and is particularly new and unknown in the United States. Most Americans have heard of quality circles (QC), usually in connection with the start up of a QC in their own organization. Interestingly enough, while most people think that the Japanese invented the QC concept, it was really part of the restoration effort of the Americans after the end of World War II. QWL differs from QC in that QWL encompasses all of the aspects of a QC but also looks at the entire working environment and does not limit itself to just technical problems as do the QC programs. Pratzner and Russell published a paper in 1984 on the development of QWL for use in vocational education programs. Their report limited itself to two major items, the implications of QWL developments for the content and instructional processes of vocational education, and what new participative management techniques may do to improve the nation's educational delivery system. The primary thrust of the article is that educational needs to learn from industry and modify the QWL techniques that have worked in industry to the educational setting. It is the firm belief of Pratzner and Russell that QWL may not necessarily be the panacea for all of the educational problems that are currently facing schools, but that in these days of eroding tax revenues, any technique that will allow the better and/or more efficient use of the available dollars should be earnestly studied.

The primary indicators of quality of work life include the accident rate, sick leave usage, employee turnover and grievances filed (Balch & Blanck, 1989). Another way to measure QWL is to perform or take an organizational survey.

Everyone has opinions, who is the best rock group, what is the best color for your house or car, where the best place is to go for the best (or worst) meal, vacation and so on. People also have opinions about work, about their job, the condition of their work environment and their relationships with their co-workers and managers. People are more than willing to share these feelings with their supervisors as long as they are assured that there will be no retaliation by management or supervision. Increased communication between the workers and management increases employee morale, helps reduce on-the-job accidents and increases productivity. In short, increases the quality of life in the work environment (QWL). Conversely, as the quality of the work life decreases, there will also be a decline in productivity, quality of work and in relationships between the workers and management.

In order to have a functional, productive QWL program, management must be firmly behind the effort, supporting and being supportive of the efforts of the workers and lower level management. As the management team shows its willingness to open up an avenue for communication by investing time and effort in an employee survey and then takes the responsibility to implement the suggestions derived from the survey, employees will be more willing to communicate their feelings and suggestions to their supervisors and managers, increasing productivity and the employee's feeling of job involvement and self control.

Most surveys gather data about job performance or indicators or predictors of job performance, but in order for a survey to be useful for QWL purposes, it must gather data on the employee's perceptions, how the employee perceives the various facets of the work environment.

In order to institute a QWL program, you must look at the way the employees think about their work environment, what is wrong with it and what is right, and one of the easiest ways to do this is to do an employee survey.

One of the biggest problems facing unionized employers and unions today is the resistance to change that they both experience when they present new and novel ways of doing things to the other party. Savage, in 1984, examined a joint quality of work life (QWL) program established by two management/union committees, composed of a municipality, a local university, and a union local. The initial agreement stated that this was to be a 24 month experiment funded with federal grant money. By the end of the grant (1978), the program was going so well that the decision was made to continue the program using both union and management funds. One of the primary focus points of the QWL committee was decision making, and by the use of joint decision making between the various involved parties, there was a "buying in" mind set that allowed changes to occur that were thought to be impossible at the introduction of the QWL program.

Many upper management people still think that the way to an employee's heart is by making the work place look better. This, however, only enhances the physical setting and does nothing to address the real problems with the work place, relationships between co-workers and supervisors and the work flow processes. The Naval Public Works Center (NPWC) in Oakland, CA focused on one (1) element of quality of work life to improve the relationship between workers and their supervisors (Bertrand, 1992). A survey in the 1989 *Federal Employees News Digest* reported that there was a large segment of the federal service employees who felt that morale had bottomed out. Out of nearly 10,000 employees surveyed, nearly 73% rated management's responsiveness as fair to poor.

To combat this problem, an ad-hoc QWL committee was formed, consisting of 10 persons, ranging from secretarial staff to engineers and an architect. The group was not only diverse by occupation but also by sex, race and length of employment. Weekly two (2) hour meetings were scheduled for 10 consecutive weeks, and each member was allowed the opportunity for input. In order to insure that outside input would be available, the meeting was open to interested parties and the site moved to different buildings to give other employees a chance to hear and be heard. It readily became obvious that the traditional "chain-of-command" information flow would not suffice in this type of an enterprise. After a number of discussions, it became apparent that meetings would also have to be scheduled with the mid-level managers for their input. As they went back to their respective work areas, the committee members acted as representatives to their co-workers.

The result of the meetings was the *QWL Accord*, an eight (8) page, pocket sized booklet that listed the committee members and the major issues that the committee felt should be addressed. Each issue was followed by the objectives, background on the objectives and a list of suggested actions. The booklet stressed that continuous improvement concepts are the key to making things happen and continue to happen. The primary purpose of the booklet was to help bridge the communication gap between the managers who made the decisions and the people who implement and have to live under them. Supervisors were encouraged to modify their behavior to bring it in line with suggested avenues and workers were encouraged to speak up and participate in the decisions that affect them.

When the booklets were distributed, the managers were advised that they should give the booklets to the employees in a group setting. During this meeting the manager should explain the background of the booklet, hand out the booklets, ask the employees to read it and listen to comments from the employees. After the employees had a chance to read and digest the material, the manager was advised to set up another meeting and discuss only the booklet and no other topics. Although no concrete examples were offered as to the programs effectiveness, Bertrand stated that the discord in the ranks was diminishing, leaving more contented employees.

JOINT DECISION MAKING

In contrast to McGregor's Theory X and Y, Owen (1987) has proposed a new addition to McGregor's two theories, namely Theory Z. Theory Z differs from either of the other two theories in that it reflects a participatory decision-making model, a reflection of the Japanese culture where it came into being. A study was performed at Illinois State University where 18 departmental chairpersons were queried as to their management style (Semlak, et al, 1986). The purpose of this study was to try and chart the current management style of a major university and plot a probable future. The results of the study exhibited some rather strange characteristics. The chairpersons, by and large, regarded their management styles as being derived from Theory Z, however, on the two most important issues (for Theory Z), they went wholeheartedly with a Theory X stance. These two issues were quality control of the product (a top priority with the Japanese), and tenure/promotion. The quality control statement that they objected to was "In my department the entire faculty feels responsible for maintaining quality teaching, research and service. We continually have discussions of how we can improve in these areas ". They felt that tenure and promotion did not arise from hard work but rather by "...getting along with key faculty members in the department." These contradictions put a large stumbling block in way of accepting that they have a Theory Z style of participatory management. A provocative point to consider here is that while industry is moving towards a Theory Z style of management, one of the leading universities in Illinois is moving towards a Theory X style of management.

EG&G Idaho National Engineering Laboratory (Ollins, 1990) decided to reveal what they felt were the underlying principles to their group problem solving approach that works! They have defined their approach as Opportunity Assessment and Planning (OAP), and it follows three phases. In the first phase, they focus on planning, while during the second they select a function, analyze the function into activity components and identify improvement opportunities. The third phase is implementation and follow up.

Phase I starts by defining goals and objectives, such as reducing frustrations, improving communications and so on. The Industrial Engineer acts as the facilitator for the group and schedules the meetings, makes sure that appropriate supplies are there and encourages management to attend the group meetings to help increase communication between the groups and management, thereby helping to clarify the issues and show that there is management support. During the meetings, the group develops mission statement(s) which focus on identifying requirements and improving services.

Phase II is the Opportunity Assessment phase. The group participants lists the functions to consider and then select the functions that will show the greatest improvement in quality or process, greatest frustration level or has the greatest impact on company resources. When this has been completed, the functions are then broken down into activity components. These components are made as specific as possible and listed in order. Once the components have been listed, the group then defines and ranks possible inhibitors (things that could interfere with the successful completion of the project), and success factors.

Phase III finds the groups developing action plans to neutralize the inhibitors, looking first at the inhibitors that have the greatest influence on cost, quality or productivity. The initial meeting results in the identified problems, responsibilities for the parts of the project, the project's scope and a tentative schedule for the project. Subsequent group meetings focus on what has been accomplished since the last meeting as well as reviewing the inhibitors, insuring that they are or have been neutralized by the action plans. Any problems are discussed and if necessary, new action plans are developed if the inhibitors are still causing problems.

Throughout EG&G's process, the Industrial Engineer (IE) is the facilitator. The IE starts and ends the meetings, introduces the participants, discusses the agenda and outlines how the meeting will be conducted. The meetings are limited to no more than two (2) hours.

Other organizations use facilitators in similar ways, but most do not necessarily use industrial engineers. Some people may argue that using an IE is wasteful when they could be doing other things, but at EG&G, it is hard to argue with a solid plan that turns out successful project after successful project.

Worker participation in decision making has often been touted as a "cure-all" for labor related problems. Lloyd and Rehg (1983), investigated the quality circle concept, which is considered by many to be one of the cornerstones of participative management. They chose the area of vocational education to examine what should be done to insure that quality circles were as successful as possible.

The authors suggested that a quality circle course be included during the final year of education and that the course be based upon the practical applications of the quality circle process. The first skills to be taught were those of management and leadership, supplemented by goal setting and conflict resolution. As the students enter the third and fourth quarters, they would find themselves tackling such issues as QC problem solving methodology, team building, statistical quality control, simulation and process implementation techniques. The final result would be a student with the practical and theoretical tools that would enable them to successfully implement a quality circle program.

The subcommittee on Federal Services commissioned a report for various agencies to consider when designing and implementing employee involvement programs ("Employee Involvement" 1988). The key points of employee involvement programs that were noted were derived from an extensive study of the experiences of both private and federal employers. One of the most important factors to be addressed when considering the institution of an employee involvement program is management interest and support. The authors of this study, along with a number of other researchers, feel that without management interest and support for an employee involvement program, it is doomed from the start. Other key concepts to weigh include a readiness assessment, communications, training, and evaluation. A readiness assessment is necessary since a number of employee involvement efforts have failed simply through the lack of readiness, a case of trying to run before they could walk. Communications within and throughout an organization is always critical but especially when the organization is attempting to involve employees in the decision making process. Another common problem for employee involvement programs is the lack of training in the essential techniques needed for staying on task and assuring that everyone is involved to the maximum extent. The last, but possibly the most important part of an employee involvement program is a continual evaluation. This is imperative to establish that progress is being made towards the original goals. The report summarized its findings by stating that each of these salient points must be present or the final product will probably not reach fruition.

Another study also examined participative management in an educational setting. Robinson (1976) chose to examine the 675 teachers were given a questionnaire that dealt with each person's input into the decision making in the school system. The results of this study showed that the principals believe that the teachers have a greater role in the decision making than the teachers perceive that they do, and the teachers believe that the principal's role in decision making is greater than the principals themselves perceive it to be. Robinson feels that by increasing the amount of participative management in the schools, the levels of teacher job satisfaction and organizational productivity will also rise.

Branst and Dubberly (1988) examined an experimental participatory management experiment that was conducted at NUMMI. NUMMI stands for New United Motor Manufacturing Inc., a joint venture between the General Motors Corporation and Toyota Motor Corporation. This venture was to see if Toyota manufacturing techniques could be "transplanted" to the United States with its unionized work force. In 1983, the UAW and NUMMI signed an agreement in which the union would support the new production system that was planned by the firm in return for the company recognizing the UAW as the sole bargaining agent for the workers. As part of the hiring process, each potential employee had to pass a three (3) day assessment that included production simulations, individual and group discussions, written tests and interviews. All new employees had to go through a four (4) day orientation process that explained the concepts that the plant was run along, including the team concept, production systems and quality principles, to name a few. One of the key ideas in the NUMMI plant was that each operator in the system had the power to stop the flow of work, that is, had decision making authority about whether or not to allow the product to continue in its current state or stop everything, allowing changes to be made to improve it or bring it back within established tolerances if it was out. While the NUMMI plant did not have quality circles, it used team meetings to accomplish the same purpose. Unlike quality circles, who are frequently focused only one or two issues, the team members can discuss anything of interest, including quality, machine set up, etc. The result of this "experiment" was that as productivity rose, the number of grievances dropped. George Nano, Chairman of the Bargaining Committee, said that there are fewer grievances because there are fewer problems. "...management supports those conditions that the union has bargained for-good and safe working conditions...".

A. O. Smith is an automotive parts manufacturer that makes frames and other structural components for automobiles and trucks, also experimented with participative management. In 1981, the company asked that its unionized steel workers allow the company to freeze 65¢ of the cost of living allowance in order to help make the company more competitive. The union agreed to the company's proposal, on the condition that the company would make some needed changes. By 1982, the company had started a quality circle program, the use of SPC, and quality improvement efforts with its major vendors. During the 1983 negotiations, the company agreed to seek professional assistance in setting up an effective problem-solving system that would involve labor and management at all levels. The consultant hired, Participative Systems, Inc., helped the company and the union develop the B.E.S.T. plan. The B.E.S.T. program has three (3) major elements, a policy committee, an advisory committee and teams. The policy committee is comprised of senior management members, leaders of all unions in the shop, and senior staff. It established overall policy and plans the joint labor/management problem-solving process. The advisory committees are composed of operations middle management, union officials, stewards, technical supervisors and informal work group leaders. Their purpose is to develop plant-wide improvement plans and are responsible for plant-level problem solving, providing support and information to the shop floor teams. The teams are the core of the effort, actively seeking out and analyzing problems, and proposing and implementing solutions. Since going to the B.E.S.T approach, the company has seen an increase in the quality of product it turns out and better labor/ management working relationship than it had in the past.

One of the primary constituents of a good participative management system is participation in the decision making process. Steve (1984) was commissioned to identify career development needs for students entering the National Institute for the Deaf. One of the most essential ingredients for success that he found was decision making/problem solving. In his paper, the various models and concepts of participative management were reviewed, including ideas and views by Heppner (1978), Greeno (1978), Bruner (1956), and others

The conclusion of the paper was that decision making/problem solving was one of the primary keys to success, however, the process of decision making/problem solving is not an instinctive procedure, but rather something that each person must be trained in order to insure that they have the fundamental tools and strategies in order to successfully solve a problem by devising and implementing a solution.

CONFLICT RESOLUTION

Another problem facing organizations is conflict, how to manage and resolve it. In 1983, the New Mexico Research and Study Council performed an analysis of the results of conflict within an organization, how to best manage them so that they are productive rather than counterproductive. To do this, they listed the various sources of organizational conflict, reactions of the participants and observers, and conflict resolution strategies. The study's authors believe that conflict can be a valuable addition to the organization as long as the managers/ administrators can effectively respond to the conflict using the proper techniques including increasing inter-group interactions, development of superordinate goals, and organizational restructuring.

INCREASED JOB SATISFACTION

Another aspect of participative management was analyzed in 1985 by Fish and Adams, by comparing the size of the organization with its management style and the job satisfaction of the Program Directors associated with each of the respondent television stations. Questionnaires were sent to 274 randomly selected stations with a return rate of 66.1% (181). The results of the survey revealed that as the stations grew larger in size, they were more likely to use a participative style of management, and that Program Directors who were oriented towards higher levels of management were more likely to express greater job satisfaction than those who were not oriented to higher levels of management.

Unlike Beehr and Gupta (1982), Gaziano and Coulson (1987) did not find that a "looser" style of management promoted job satisfaction among employees. They examined two newspapers that were owned by the same company, a morning paper and an evening paper. The 125 journalists that were polled using a 12 page survey rated the morning paper as a blend of "democratic and authoritarian" while the evening paper was considered to be authoritarian. The results of the survey were that the journalists on both papers felt that their participation in decision making was important, but the employees at the morning paper (democratic/authoritative) were no more likely to participate in decision making than the employees of the more formal evening paper. In fact, there was more satisfaction found in the working relationships between the journalists and the editors at the evening paper than at the morning paper. The factors which caused this "difference" from what was expected are unknown, but the authors suspect that it may have to do with the fact that journalists tend to be more transient than other professionals.

INCREASED COOPERATION

There have been major developments over the course of time in labor-management relations, especially in the area of cooperation. There have been many changes in the direction of negotiations between unions and the management. Two of the most profound changes have been the cooperation between unions and management, and cooperation between management and the individual employees. McCabe (1984) performed an integrative analysis on these two aspects of cooperation between labor and management in an effort to help balance the overwhelming glowing reports of participative management that usually manage to either gloss over or ignore the negative features of participative management. The final point of his analysis is that cooperation and participative management are not ventures that can be put into place immediately and yield instantaneous results, but rather need to be introduced slowly over a protracted length of time.

PRODUCTIVITY

In a report on union-management cooperation prepared for the W. E. Upjohn Institute by M. H. Schuster (1984), the author examined a number of organizations over a five year period with the primary focus of the study being improved productivity. One of the sections of this study dealt with a comparison between Scanlon plans and Quality Circles. Some people use the two terms interchangeably, they are, however, not the same thing. Scanlon plans are the "brainchild" of Joseph Scanlon, a cost accountant and United Steel Workers union official. During the mid 1930's, Scanlon devised a plan where a formula was devised to help share the profits with all of a company's employees. This approach encouraged increased union-management cooperation that changed their previous adversarial working arrangement to one where the main focus was aimed at reducing costs and increasing output (Moore and Ross, 1987).

Quality Circle committees usually involve more people than Scanlon committees, rewards for suggestions usually are distributed between the members of the circle whereas the Scanlon plans distribute the savings over the entire work force, and last, the author notes that most companies who establish Quality Circles are more likely to maintain traditional, authoritarian views on employee participation and involvement.

A survey commissioned by the Association for Quality and Participation (Stuebing, 1995) was conducted by the Center for Effective Organizations (it is directed by E. E. Lawler III). It researched the idea that managers in the United States are somewhat reluctant to share power with the employees. A 16 page survey was sent to 985 companies from the *FORTUNE* 1,000 list of the nation's largest manufacturers, though only 279 companies responded. The results showed that 1) 37% are not participating in employee involvement activities, 2) 31% of the employees are responsible for making recommendations to management but do not have the necessary resources to help them make the decisions, 3) 12% of the employees that are on participative teams only receive information that directly relates to their tasks, 4) only 10% of the employees are heavily involved and receive the necessary training and information on the company and its competitors.

It was further reported that companies that had "high involvement" (at least 40-60% of the employees) with power sharing programs consistently outperformed companies that exhibited "low involvement" (20% of the employees or less).

The educational and organizational strategies required for improvement of worker-centered productivity was the subject of a paper by Drewes (1982). Drewes felt that unless a person was able to accurately assess productivity, there could be no meaningful decision on whether or not changes that were made in the organization were actually part of the solution and not an additional part of the cause. The equation developed was that productivity equals the output (system products) divided by the input (resources used). Using this equation, it is easily understood that increased productivity could be caused by any of the following: a) an increase in the overall output (input remaining constant), b) a decrease in the resources used (output remaining constant), c) an increase in the output with a simultaneous decrease in the input, d) a larger increase in the output than in the input, and finally, e) a smaller decrease in the output than is found in the input. These five different scenarios must be considered whenever there is a major change in the organizational philosophy, such as the introduction of a participative management system. Drewes felt that there are four vital ingredients to successful productivity improvement, information distribution, communication between individuals, a mutual understanding and general consensus as to what the problem to be tackled is, and finally, involvement of all parties. All of these issues must be addressed through increased education of the involved workers into how to function as a team and open the channels of communication, therefore it becomes vitally important that a participative management program is not just installed in place without adequate training for all workers as to its function and purpose.

Although participative management systems appear to be the solution to many of today's organizational work problems, one of the main factors to be concerned about is productivity. If the productivity stays constant while the costs go up, the organization will eventually go bankrupt and close, causing catastrophic dislocations among its employees. In a study performed under the auspices of the U.S. General Accounting Service, 36 firms who had installed productivity sharing plans and nine who were either considering or had rejected productivity sharing plans were interviewed. The results showed that 34 of the 36 firms with plans currently in place detected an increase in productivity after the plans were initiated and were going to continue to use the plans. There were two firms that were unhappy with the plans in place. One firm had been increasing the amount of automation that was associated with the job, reducing the potential of the workers to affect production. The other company had come to feel that money was no longer a good incentive for the workers and was planning to institute a Quality of Work Life (QWL) program to replace its productivity sharing plan. On the whole, it appears that productivity sharing plans, such as Scanlon, Rucker, and Improshare, do have a positive effect on the productivity of the employees.

Previously, Frost, Wakely, and Ruh (1974) performed a rather intensive look at Scanlon plans, what they were, how they were used, what were the advantages and pitfalls. Their analysis of the Scanlon plan showed an increase in communication and an increase in productivity, however, a noticeable defect in their study was that the productivity increase was never examined for short or long term negative effects, such as short term increased costs, or long term losses due to increased costs, etc. One negative side effect that did turn up was that in several cases, increased productivity did not result in increased profits for the company which could be passed on to the employees as bonuses. This had soured the participating employees on any sort of participative management style profit-sharing plan.

Harry Schmerl, the Assistant Chief Civil Engineer for the Port Authority of New York and New Jersey (1989) reported on a plan by the Port Authority to improve productivity through a Participative Measurement Process (PMP). Measurements and goals were developed for each of the "representative groups", a team of from eight (8) to twelve (12) employees. Each team represented a cross section of the unit, consisting of darfters, designers, engineers, and administrative and clerical personnel. Meetings were held and decisions were made by group consensus. The results of this project were that each unit's productivity index out-performed its projected improvement rate. The reasons for this were that as time went on, more of the staff began to take an interest in the project and gained a better understanding of it, a greater commitment was made to keeping more timely records, resulting in budget and schedule adjustments, more projects received postmortem examinations, revealing design and implementation strengths and weaknesses, and more time was spent in communicationg with the clients, making it easier to clarify their needs and wants and incorporate those needs and wants in the projects. All in all, by increasing communication and empowering the employees involved in the various projects, the Port Authority realized a real increase in productivity.

Beehr and Gupta (1982), examined two automotive supply organizations which were similar in both size and level of technology used to conduct business, but differed in managerial style. One plant was high unionized and therefore had a very rigid hierarchical structure while the other plant used a modified Scanlon plan (Frost, Wakely, & Ruh, 1974). The results of the study showed that the employees at the unionized plant had a greater level of stress then the employees of the plant that utilized the modified Scanlon plan, which manifested itself not only in the measures taken through structured interviews, but was also seen in the fact that the absenteeism was approximately 4 times greater in the unionized plant. This difference is significant, however, Beehr and Gupta (1982) did not mention analyzing the union contract to determine whether or not the contract language might have inadvertently lead to increased absenteeism. The final conclusion of this study was that the work environment was less stressful for the "rank and file" but more stressful for the managerial staff in the organization where participative management was used.

Steven Pejovich (1984) presents a contrasting point of view concerning participative management as he depicts the style of partic-ipative management as it is practiced in four different countries, West Germany, Norway, Ireland, and the United States. Pejovich carefully outlines the conditions under which participative management existed in the study's population, and then proceeded to show the underlying assumptions that have been used for the rationale for the styles found. In West Germany, several laws have been enacted to insure that the labor groups represent approximately half of the entire board of direc-tors in all companies that have over 2,000 employees. Norway has gone even further into mandatory participative management by de-creeing that labor participation in small firms (less than 50 employees) are subject to voluntary negotiations, medium sized firms (50-200 employees) must allow the employees to elect up to one third of the board if 50% of the employees so desire, and it is mandatory that large firms (greater than 200 employees) have one third of the board comprised of employees. Another interesting feature of Norway's attitude towards participative management is that local governments are not asking for a direct board representation.

Ireland, in 1977, passed the Worker Participation Act which mandated, in a fashion similar to Norway's provisions, that one third of all boards of directors must be composed of employees who are employed with the specific company whose board they are on.

At the present time, participative management in the United States is primarily a joint voluntary effort between the workers (or unions) and the management. Signs of mandatory employee involve-ment are beginning to be seen in the statements of participative management proponents, whose primary argument for the passage of laws is that this would replace conflict between labor and management with cooperation. In fact, in the countries where such laws have been passed, it appears that the board usually divides itself into two camps, stockholders and employees. Prior to each full board session, each of the groups meet to discuss and map out strategy for the next meeting. This turns the board meetings into negotiation sessions rather than incubators for ideas. One critical issue is the problem of confidentiality, and evidence from West Germany suggests that the employee board members have leaked essential information to the unions during wage negotiations.

The prime premise of this study is that if participative management produces such excellent results, then why does it have to be legislated, since companies are usually willing to try almost anything that will positively affect the bottom line?

Edward Glaser (1973) spent considerable time gathering case studies of organizations concerned with participative management. In a number of these studies, the organization was floundering, apparently ready to collapse at any moment when the upper level management decided to try using a participative management approach to try and ward off the demise of the organization. In each case, the company turned around and began to be profitable, or became more profitable. In each of the case histories that were presented, the underlying theme was that of a joint effort in problem solving and decision making between the management and workers.

Some early research by Milutinovich, et al, (1971) into job satisfaction and group cohesiveness was performed using race as one of the discriminant variables. Using the Job Descriptive Index, Seashore's measure of group cohesiveness, and Likert's Profile of Organizational Characteristics, the researchers found that there was little differences between white and black workers in that they both preferred a participative style of management to the more structured styles and this was reflected in higher job satisfaction, greater group cohesiveness, increased pay, and increased number of promotions. In summation, race appeared to play little if any part at all in terms of job satisfaction and other measures of work group stability. In fact, the more participative the style of management was, the more likely the workers were to have increased job satisfaction.

Educational institutions should be on the cutting edge of new ideas, but in 1978, S. A. Prewitt found out differently. Likert's Profile of Organizational Characteristics was sent out to a random sample of administrative employees from the 31 educational institutions that make up the Southern Association of Colleges and Schools (each of the schools in the sample had to have bachelors, masters, and doctoral programs). The results of the study indicated that nearly all of the administrative employees felt that their school's style of management fell somewhere within the domain of consultative style. Interestingly enough, none of the respondents felt that their institution should be ranked as tending towards a participative management style on any of the twenty questions asked.

David Nash (1985) performed a similar study using dental colleges in the United States. The deans, associate deans, and departmental chairs of the 60 U.S. dental colleges were given a survey that consisted of a modified version of Likert's Profile of Organizational Characteristics. The results of the survey showed that there was very little difference between the results obtained by Prewitt in his study and the placement of the dental colleges. Both schools tended to be in the consultative style of management with occasional tendencies towards a benevolent authoritarian format.

Considerable work and study has been given to the topic of Scanlon plans and participative management, and one of the acknowledged experts in the field C. F. Frost, coauthored a book on this matter with J. H. Wakely and R. A. Ruh (1974). According to Frost, et al, all sharing plans, Scanlon not withstanding, must have four basic underlying principles, an identity, participation by employees, chance of equity (that is, an equitable return on their invest of ideas, energy, competence and commitment), and finally, managerial competence. Frost felt that even if the three other principles were in use, the plans would ultimately fail if managerial competence was not present. Basically, the authors felt that if employees believed that management was incompetent and that decisions were irrational, then they would lose confidence in management and their cooperation and work would suffer. Additional work by Taylor and Cangemi (1983), confirmed the suppositions and principles set forth by Frost, et al.

In 1980, Daniel Zwerdling collected a series of case histories on participative management, when it worked, and when it did not. In every case where participative management styles were introduced, there were some immediate changes for the better, however, in some instances, the changes that were wrought reverted back to the previous unacceptable circumstances. In each instance where there was a failure, it could be easily seen that much of the failure was due to the fact that there was more lip service than actual follow through. This caused the employees to become discontented with their jobs, and thus affected the organization's productivity. The main point that was driven home was that if a company plans to introduce a participative management style, they must invest both the time and effort necessary to make it work, including the retraining of traditional authoritarian managers and educating the employees themselves. Without firm backing from upper management, including free flowing communications from the top to the bottom and back, any attempt to introduce participative management will fail and could actually make things worse than what they may currently be.

Hewlett-Packard is considered by many experts to be a forerunner in the effort to effectively train and develop its management team (Nilsson, 1984). The fundamental essence of the Hewlett-Packard program is that each employee is involved in the company from their first day. They are instructed in the "HP Way," the methods of corporate communication, decision making/problem solving, and continuing training, to insure that they understand what to expect and what is expected of them. These "rules of conduct" and corporate philosophy are stressed through each training course and orientation, including those given to senior corporate executives. The result is that the channels of communication flow freely from the bottom to the top of the corporate structure as well as within each level. This "whole corporation" approach has encouraged the employees to challenge each other and the company to constantly improve on what they have, striving for the optimal payback on each dollar spent.

The Duluth Minnesota Public Schools were in trouble in the early 1980's, as evidenced by teacher strikes and employee relations benchmarks such as absenteeism and turnover (Moeser & Golen, 1987). In 1984, the school board decided to improve management and employee relations by instituting a participative management plan. The plan stressed communication between the various levels of the system as the best way to achieve results. The board went on to establish a participative management policy, rules and regulations, a structure for communication and sharing of ideas, and a budget for the process. The results of the program showed that prior to institution of the plan, 152 grievances were filed, however, in the first semester of the 1986-87 school year, only nine were filed. The authors feel that the reduction in grievances is just the tip of the employee relations iceberg, that there is vastly improved communications between the various organizational groups and many problems that would have been grieved earlier are now being jointly resolved through the participative management process.

Three school districts were the focus of a paper that investigated the concept of team management (Anderson, 1988). The team management approach, as outlined by the author, is a participative management system that involves the upper level administrators and excludes the middle level administrators and teachers. One of the key principles of the team management approach is that nearly all of the decisions are a result of team consensus. Although this requires taking longer to reach a decision, each of the school districts found that adding the extra time to the beginning of a project shortened the implementation time and caused fewer problems than had occurred with a "top down" decision.

Harris (1986) proposes three different leadership styles, the manager-as-technician, manager-as-conductor, and manager-as developer, similar to the leadership styles expounded upon by Bradford and Cohen in their book *Managing for Excellence* (1984). Basically, the manager-as-technician is the manager who has been promoted up the ladder to the present position. The manager got to the position by excelling in some area that is linked to the position. An example of this would be promoting the top salesman to the position of sales training manager, the supposition being that the best salesman is doing the right things, therefore, the person must also know how they did it and can teach those skills to others. The manager-as-conductor is an unfortunate offshoot of the participative management theory, that is, the manager's prime goal is to try and work through the employees, in other words, to control the individuals under them and make certain that they perform the correct actions. The problem with both this and the manager-as-technician styles is that both force the subordinates to rely on the manager's direction, knowledge, and planning, thereby stunting the potential growth of the subordinates. The third style, manager-as-developer, is the true inheritor of the participative management mantle. These managers share the responsibility with their employees and attempt to "develop" the team approach. This leads to the influx of new ideas and methods to deal with problems that the organization may face. In concluding his arguments, the author states that being able to effectively manage "change" is the basic leadership requirement, and in this light, the manager-as-developer is the most effective style.

Most people confuse leading with managing, or feel that the two terms are synonymous. Leading is defined by Webster as the act of showing someone the way, while managing is defined as influencing a person so that that person does what the "manager" wants. The crucial word which clearly distinguishes between the two is "influencing". Thomas Harris (1987) conducted a poll of randomly selected non-Fortune 500 companies in the state of Indiana who had an annual sales of at least $5,000,000. The CEOs or presidents of each company polled were surveyed about situational leadership using Hershey and Blanchard's Leadership Effectiveness and Adaptability Description (LEAD). The results of the study indicated that the managers favored a management style that was high task and high relationship, and almost entirely neglecting the delegation of responsibility to subordinates. The most interesting feature of the results is that although the managers used a "hands on" style of management, their perception of themselves was as a manager-as developer.

Wongruangwisan (1980) studied managerial leadership style and organizational effectiveness by examining all privately owned manufacturing companies in Bangkok which employed at least 1,000 persons (total size of the population which met these criteria was 53). The random sample of 10 organizations was drawn from this pool, and questionnaires were sent to each of the upper four levels of the management, the top manager, the department manager, a supervisor, and three workers (the supervisor and workers were randomly selected from each department within the company. The results of the study showed that the most common type of management could be placed between the benevolent authoritative and consultative. It was also found that the higher up in the organization a person was, the more likely they were to practice participative management. Another hypothesis examined by the study was that there was a positive relationship between the management system and the organizational effectiveness, which proved to be true. The final hypothesis tested by this study was that there was a direct relationship between the educational level of the department manager and the organizational effectiveness. The null hypothesis was rejected because the obtained values did not exceed critical values, however, the very small difference between the obtained and critical values indicated that additional research should be conducted on the relationship between a department manager's educational level and organizational effectiveness.

Richard T. Harley (1993) is an employee involvement expert. He and his company have helped save their clients *over 1.4 billion dollars* by convincing the companies to go to their employees and listen to suggestions. A large wood product producing client of his company used a suggestion from the employees that the wood chips, dust and shavings be sold to local nurseries as mulch, thus turning a liability into another product line and profit making asset. Mr. Harley contends that increased productivity and profits can be made by listening to your employees since they are involved in the production process intimately all day long.

In 1982, Edward E. Lawler III, created a position paper on the relationship between education, management style, and organizational effectiveness. One study that was cited was a study of the educational levels of managers which revealed that 49% of the managers who were under 40 had MBAs while only 16% of the managers who were 50-59 had MBAs. Other points that were made (supported by research) were that the more education an employee has, the more likely they are to want participative management; there is little hard data on any relationship between level of education and productivity; there is very little empirical research on organizations who have radically changed their style of management; there is little research on the effectiveness of high involvement systems (participative management); and most arguments that favor a switch to participative management rely heavily on comparative studies and on linking societal change to work place change. His closing statements argue for more research in the area of organizational effectiveness and productivity with a participative style of management.

Doucoulinagos (1993) analyzed the results of 43 published studies to investigate the effects on productivity by worker participation in decision making and profit sharing, as well as a number of other variables. His results showed that if worker participation in decision making is mandated by the government, it tends to be counterproductive. In firms where it occurred but was not mandated, productivity increased. Profit sharing showed a strong positive association with productivity in labor managed firms (LMF), but was weaker in participatory capitalist firms (PCF).

Another variable that was examined was mandated codeterminism, however, there was a negative association between mandated codeterminism and productivity.

SUMMARY

A review of the available literature shows that participative management is not just one single, simple concept. Rather, it is an integration of at least six (6) different, but related concepts, Leadership, Motivation, Communication, Goals, Decision and Control.

Studies have been performed in a number of organizations, both private and public, and in both the "for profit" and "non-profit" types. There have been some studies that touched on the question of whether or not participative styles of management increased actual efficiencies of the organization, but none of them directly addressed this issue.

This study directly attempted to explore the issue of increased productivity as a direct result of the use of participative styles of management.

III

DESIGN AND METHODOLOGY

DESIGN OF THE STUDY

This study was designed to examine the relationship between the style of management that an organization uses and its profitability using Likert's Profile of Organizational Characteristics (a standardized survey) to define the style of management used and the Dun & Bradstreet financial rating of the organization to help define profitability, the underlining premise being that a company with high productivity is more likely to be profitable. The two terms (productivity and profitable) are not interchangeable, because the ability to bring about a desired outcome (productivity) is not the same as obtaining a financial gain or benefit (profitable), since something can be productive without being profitable, such as in the case of a child cleaning their room. A child cleaning their room will be productive for the parent from a time management point of view, but will not necessarily yield a financial gain for either the parent or the child. A number of different variables were examined through the use of a demographic section that was added to the Profile of Organizational Characteristics (Appendix E). The demographic variables were included to help determine whether any differences in the management style ratings between companies or between individuals within the companies could be due to inconsistencies that were previously noted in earlier research. The variables that were investigated are (a) the age of the top level managers (Hypothesis III); (b) the educational level of the top level managers (Hypothesis I); (c) the sex of the top level managers (to determine if there is two terms (productivity and profitable) are not interchangeable, because difference between female and male responses); (d) the age of the organization (Hypothesis II); and (e) the size of the organization in terms of both number of employees and the number of buildings it uses (Hypothesis IV). The data used for the fifth hypothesis were taken from the Dun & Bradstreet ratings and compared to the organizational mean response on Likert's Profile of Organizational Characteristics.

PARTICIPANTS IN THE STUDY

The participants in the study were all officers of organizations that manufacture office furniture in the United States of America, taken from Dun & Bradstreet's *Million Dollar Directory*, further identified by having an Standard Industrial Classification code of 2521 or 2522. A SIC Code of 2521 denotes a company that produces metal office furniture while a SIC Code of 2522 is for organizations that produce wood office furniture. These codes are by no means exclusive, and a company could be registered under both. Financial data on the responding organizations was taken from the most recent Dun & Bradstreet ratings.

INSTRUMENTATION

Each subject was sent a letter stating the purpose of the study along with a copy of a modified version of Likert's Profile of Organizational Characteristics. The survey assessed six key elements (leadership, motivation, communication, decisions, goals, and control) used to differentiate between exploitive, benevolent, consultative, and participative styles of management. Demographic questions were added at the end of the survey to help more fully characterize the responses received and test the hypotheses. These questions included the number of full time employees, the number of work sites (separate buildings, the age of the organization, the level of the respondent in the organization, how many persons there were on the respondents level, the respondent's educational level, their sex and finally, their age.

Likert's Profile of Organizational Characteristics (POC), is comprised of six sections, Leadership (questions 1-3), Motivation (4-6), Communication (7-10), Decisions (11 and 12), Goals (13 and 14) and Control (15 and 16). Each of these questions was compared not only to each of the nine demographic questions and the two financial factors, but also to each other (Appendices E and F).

The POC currently has three different forms, Form J, Form S and a modified version of Form S. A split half reliability on Forms J and S usually result in values of +0.90 to +0.96. This study used

Form S, which has been in use since 1977 and in a great number of studies, a number of them performed by the Institute for Social Research at the University of Michigan. J. M. Ketchel (1972), in a doctoral dissertation study, examined management styles in 17 counties that comprised the mid-Ohio Health Planning Federation. Ketchel received 158 completed responses from 16 different counties and correlated the mean total scores for each county with the performance for that county. The correlation between the POC mean score and the member rating of county effectiveness was +0.83, while the correlation for POC mean score and member scaled expectancy rating was +0.74.

There have been a number of studies conducted in Japan, Yugoslavia and the United States, to name some of the better known studies, and in each case there was a distinct difference between the scores on the POC and the dependent variable, production output. In the Japanese studies (two were cited with numbers for comparison purposes), a *t* test was performed to determine whether or not there were significant differences in the styles between production units which were doing well and production units which were not doing well. The results showed a t_{obt} of -7.56 with a t_{crit} of 4.30 at the $\alpha = 0.05$ level with two degrees of freedom.

Basically, the high productivity plant had a style of management that was different from the style of the low productivity plant, as measured by the POC. The researchers concluded that since the plants used similar equipment, produced the same product and were the same size, that at least in the plants studied, a participative style of management was more conducive to productivity.

COLLECTION OF DATA

Surveys were sent to the individuals identified in all organizations in the United States with the SIC 2521 and/or 2522, identified in Dun & Bradstreet's *Million Dollar Directory*. Each individual that the survey was sent to was assigned a specific four digit identification code that appeared on the upper right hand corner of the survey. The individuals who received the questionnaire were asked to complete it within a two week period from date of receipt and return it via the self addressed, stamped envelope (the assumption was made that it would have taken no more than one week from date of mailing to receive the letter). Sixty days after the initial letters were sent out, telephone calls were made to those individuals who had not responded to the written request.

No more than two telephone calls were made to any listed individual. If the individual indicated during the first call that they were not interested in filling out the survey, they were thanked for their time and the conversation was ended. If the person indicated that they had not received the survey, they were sent another survey. If the person indicated that they had received the survey but had not gotten around to filling it out, they were asked to please complete it and return it as soon as possible.

Only those individuals who stated that they were going to complete the survey during the first telephone conversation received a second call, approximately 30 days after the first call. No additional calls were made after the second attempt, the assumption being that if a written request and two telephone calls failed to get a response, another telephone call would likewise be ignored.

ANALYSIS OF DATA

The responses were individually keyed into the computer, care being taken to insure that members of the same organizations would be joined together for an average organizational response in the final analyses. Means were calculated for each question to determine whether or not there were any inconsistencies with regards to previously reported studies involving the POC. Correlational analyses were performed on each of the questions on the questionnaire. Due to the fact that Factor 24 dealt with the sex of the respondent, point biserial correlations were performed when there was a comparison between Factor 24 and any other factor. Additional correlational analyses were performed utilizing the various sections of the POC (leadership, motivation, communications, decisions, goals and controls) with the various demographic questions to help determine whether or not any of the subsections of the POC correlated with any of the demographic factors better than the overall POC score. For each hypothesis, the null hypothesis was expressed in terms of population values of the correlation coefficients equaling zero, or symbolically represented as:

$$H_o: p(rho) = 0,$$

with a level of significance of $\alpha = 0.05$ (two tailed test). Correlations were considered only if their absolute value was equal to or exceeded 0.30, due to the fact that a correlation of 0.30 will account for nearly 10 % of the variance of the *Y* variable when predicted from the *X* variable and is frequently used in the social sciences as the lowest critical correlation that assumptions can be based on.

Hypothesis I

The higher the educational level of the organization's managers is, the more likely they are to use a participative management style of management.

Within responding organization, the responses from each person responding were averaged and the averages used in a Pearson Product Moment Correlation. A positive correlation greater than or equal to 0.30 between the educational level of the organization's respondents and the score on the POC would indicate that higher educational levels in managers result in an increased use of participative management.

Hypothesis II

The older an organization is, the less likely they are to use a participative style of management.

Within responding organization, the responses from each person responding were averaged and the averages used in a Pearson Product Moment Correlation. A negative correlation less than or equal to -0.30 between the age of the organization and the average score on the POC would indicate that younger companies are more likely to use a participative type of management than older, more established organizations.

Hypothesis III

The older the organization's managers are, the less likely they are to use a participative style of management.

Within responding organization, the responses from each person responding were averaged and the averages used in a Pearson Product Moment Correlation. A negative correlation less than -0.30 between the age of the managers and the score on the POC would indicate that older manager's are less likely to use a participative style of management.

Hypothesis IV

Organizations who use a participative style of management are more likely to be smaller in size than organizations who use a more rigid style of management.

Within responding organization, the responses from each person responding were averaged and the averages used in a Pearson Product Moment Correlation. A negative correlation less than -0.30 between the size of the organization and the score on the POC would indicate that smaller organizations are more likely to use a participative style of management than larger organizations.

Hypothesis V

Organizations that use a participative style of management will have increased productivity that will result in increased financial stability as compared to organizations that do not use a participative style of management.

Within responding organization, the responses from each person responding were averaged and the averages used in a Pearson Product Moment Correlation. A positive correlation greater than 0.30 between the financial stability of the organization and the score on the POC would indicate that a participative style of management results in increased productivity which is translated into increased financial stability. Productivity was defined in terms of financial stability for a number of reasons, the most obvious being is that financial stability is something that can be readily measured in discrete, objective units. Each company was rated on a financial stability scale that was composed of two parts, yearly sales and a financial rating from Dun & Bradstreet. Both of these factors were computed for each responding company using a linear number conversion of the factors. A number of previous studies using the POC have found that overall sales appears to be positively correlated with a high score on the POC. Yearly sales of $1,000,000 to $5,000,000 were assigned a point value of two, $6,000,000 to $10,000,000 were assigned a value of four, $11,000,000 to $25,000,000 were assigned a value six, $26,000,000 to $50,000,000 were given a value of eight, $51,000,000 to $100,000,000 were assigned a value of 10, and finally, any companies with yearly sales greater than $100,000,000 were given a value of 12.

Dun & Bradstreet rates financial stability using a five point system, with 1A being the lowest rating and 5A being the highest. Each of these financial stability ratings was doubled, resulting in the final financial stability rating being two for 1A, four for 2A, six for 3A, eight for 4A and 10 for 5A.

The numbers obtained from both parts of the financial stability indicator (yearly sales and the Dun & Bradstreet rating) were separately compared to the POC average and they were also multiplied (yearly sales times Dun & Bradstreet rating) and compared to the POC averages. The final results of the study were analyzed using the factor obtained by multiplying the yearly sales by the Dun & Bradstreet rating, increasing the spread between companies with sound financial ratings and those with below average financial ratings.

Correlational analyses were performed on all variables, including the following: averages of responses on questionnaire, age of organization, size of organization (number of employees), number of different locations, type of management style, age of top managers, educational level of top managers, and sex of top managers. Additionally, correlational analyses were performed between the demographic variables to determine whether or not there were any other demographic factors influencing the five hypotheses. The correlations were performed in order to determine whether or not any of the five hypotheses were true, or rather if the null hypothesis for each of the five hypotheses could be false. The critical value for rejecting the null hypothesis is approximately $\pm$ 0.156 (α = 0.05) for all hypotheses that do not involve the financial factors, annual sales, current financial status (rating) from Dun & Bradstreet and financial stability rating (Factors 27, 28 and 29). The critical value for rejecting the null hypothesis for These factors is $\pm$ 0.201 (α = 0.05), due to the fact that there were fewer degrees of freedom.

SUMMARY

Each of the employees listed as part of the organization's management team in the *Million Dollar Directory* within each of the targeted organizations was sent a copy of the survey instrument, Likert's Profile of Organizational Characteristics (POC), that had been supplemented with nine demographic questions. Sixty days after the surveys had been sent out, telephone contact was made with all of those individuals who had not yet responded, and another survey form was sent to them if they requested one.

The data that was received was analyzed using SPSS, Release 4.1, on an IBM Model 3090-200E mainframe computer, located at Ferris State University, Big Rapids, MI. Correlational analyses were performed on all 29 factors/question, consisting of 16 POC questions, nine demographic questions, a response average of the 16 POC questions, and three different financial statistics (annual sales, Dun & Bradstreet rating and a financial stability rating). A *t* test was performed for each of the hypotheses as well as a confidence interval for each of the pertinent correlation coefficients.

IV

RESULTS

INTRODUCTION

The purpose of this study was to determine if using a participative style of management would increase the productivity of an organization, thereby increasing its financial stability. Additionally, research was conducted to determine what demographic factors had to be present in order for an organization to use a participative style of management. Likert's Profile of Organizational Characteristics, with a demographic survey added, was sent to all of the executives listed in the Dun & Bradstreet's *Million Dollar Directory* with a self-addressed, stamped envelope for ease of return. The review of the literature in Chapter II outlined the various components of what comprised a participative style of management and how each of these components fits into the entire participative management scenario.

The results of this study, all research hypotheses and other findings of interest, are presented in this chapter. Each of the hypotheses are presented in the same order in which the were discussed in the first and second chapters.

673 surveys, complete with stamped, addressed return envelopes, were mailed with sent to the executives listed in Dun & Bradstreet's *Million Dollar Directory*, whose organizations had the SIC (Standard Industrial Classification) of 2521 or 2522. There were 138 initial responses to the survey. Follow up on non-respondents occurred 60 days after the initial mailing by telephoning the company and asking for the individual. During the telephone contact, each person who had failed to respond to the initial request was asked if they had received the survey and if they had, when would they be able to fill it out. In 18 cases, a second survey was sent to the person who stated that they had not received it. An additional 10 surveys were sent to individuals who had replaced the initial person that the survey was

originally sent to. Thirty days after the first follow up telephone calls, an additional 23 completed surveys were received. At this point, additional telephone contact resulted in no additional surveys, with the exception of one survey that was received 14 months after the initial mailings.

For the most part, surveys with low ratings were evenly distributed through the return flow of the surveys. The only exception to this occurred at the very end of the return period, after the first telephone contact, when two of the lowest rated POCs were among the last four received.

A return rate of 24% is not particularly high. The most common reason given for not returning the surveys in the time requested was that the person was too busy. Other possible participants stated that they had not received the survey or did not know where to return it. Finally, other potential respondents stated that they did not fill out surveys.

Correlational analyses on were performed on component factors of the POC to determine whether or not the POC was valid (Appendix F), in this instance, for the variables being examined. Comparisons between the various factors have been performed in other studies and the results from this study compare favorably to similar correlational analyses performed in other studies between the various components of the POC. Null hypotheses were constructed for the five hypotheses under examination in the study, using $\alpha = 0.05$, as follows:

$$H_o: p(rho) = 0 \ (\alpha = 0.05)$$

A *t* test for independent means was used to test the existence of a relationship between the level of education of the organizations's managers, the managers' ages, the size and age of the organization and the organization's financial stability and the style of management used by each responding organization. The null hypotheses (*Ho*) were:

1.   There will be no difference in the educational levels of the mangers who use a participative style of management and the managers who do not use a participative style of management.

2.   There will be no differences in the ages between organizations that use a participative style of management and organizations that do not use a participative style of management.

3. There will be no difference in age between managers who use a participative style of management and managers who do not use a participative style of management.

4. There will be no difference in size between organizations that use participative management and organizations that do not use a participative style of management.

5. There will be no difference in financial stability between organizations that use participative management and organizations that do not use participative management.

DEMOGRAPHIC CHARACTERISTICS OF THE SAMPLE

Likert's Profile of Organizational Characteristics (POC), as stated in Chapter III, contains 16 questions that relate to each other within specific groupings that help define management style. An additional nine questions concerned with the demographics of the respondent population were added at the end of the POC. Table 1 includes the information related to the demographic parameters of the respondents.

Approximately 9.3% of the respondents were female, with an average age somewhere between 41 and 45, and had slightly less than four years of college. By contrast, the male population had an average age of somewhere between 46 and 50, with slightly more than four years of college. The organizations that females worked in tended to be smaller (151-250 employees in 3 buildings) than their average male executive (500+ employees in an average of 9 buildings). The overall response average for females was 4.83 while for males it was 5.44. During the inputting of the data, it was noted that in a number of cases, female respondents appeared have lower average response ratings than males within the same organization. An analysis was then performed to determine if there was a relationship between sex and low responses on the POC. A *t* test was run on the grand mean for the females as compared to the grand mean for the males, to determine whether or not the mean of the females could be a subset of the entire study population. This can be symbolically stated as

$$H_o : \mu = 5.39 \ (\alpha = 0.05)$$

The results were $t = -1.944$ and $t_{cv} = -2.145$. The null hypothesis was not rejected at the $\alpha = 0.05$ level.

Although the null hypothesis was not rejected, further examinations were performed by separating the response averages for Level I and Level II females. Level I positions are those top executive positions that hold the title of CEO, president, etc., while Level II positions are typically vice presidents, department managers, plant managers, etc. At this point the decision was made to separate out the females who were in organizations with a Level I female and those female respondents who were in organizations where there were no Level I females. The means for the two groups were 5.7 and 4.3, respectively. Separate t tests were performed for each of the two means resulting in the following null hypotheses:

Level 1 Female Present

Hypothesis: There will be no difference in the means between females who are in an organization with a Level I female and the male response average. This null hypothesis was represented as:

$$H_o: \mu = 5.39 \ (\alpha = 0.10)$$

The results were $t = -0.782$ and $t_{cv} = \pm 1.860$. The null hypothesis not rejected, that is, the obtained t value of -0.782 does not exceed the t_{cv} value of -1.860. In other words, there is no appreciable difference between the male response average and the female response average of females in organizations where there is a Level I female (a female holds the top executive office).

Level 1 Female Not Present

Hypothesis: There will be no difference in the means between females who are in an organization with a Level I male and the male response average. This null hypothesis was represented as:

$$H_o: \mu = 5.39 \ (\alpha = 0.10)$$

The results were $t = -5.012$ and $t_{cv} = -2.015$. The null hypothesis is rejected due to the fact that the obtained t value of -5.0122 exceeds the t_{cv} value of -2.015.

It appears that females who are in organizations that do not have a female in a top level position (CEO, president, etc.) responded with lower ratings on the POC than companies who had a female in the top level (Level I).

ANALYSES RESULTS

The correlations between the 16 questions of the POC and the sub-factor average (Factor 26) ranged from 0.63 to 0.78 (see Table 2).

Factor 26 is an average of each individual's responses to all of the 16 POC questions, therefore, there should be a high correlation between the individual responses and the average of these responses. The primary purpose of performing these correlations was to check and insure the reliability and validity of the data gathered. The correlations between the various individual sub-factors ranged between 0.30 and 0.71 (Appendix B).

Additional correlational analyses were performed between the various sections (an average was taken of each of the sub-factor groups and the groups were compares to each other) of the POC, Leadership, Motivation, Communication, Goals, Decision and Control and the results are shown in Table 3.

As can be readily seen in Table 3, there are very strong, positive relationships between the various POC factors.

There were a number of correlations between the various demographic factors where it appeared that there was a relationship between the factors under consideration, shown in Table 4.

It is logical that there were fairly high correlations between the factors dealing with number of employees, work sites and age of the organization since the more employees a company has the more work space it needs to provide and as a company gets older, it expands and grows, requiring more employees.

It is also understandable that there should be a high correlation between the number of employees on the respondent's level and the number of employees on the top two levels of management. Since there are more lower level (2nd echelon) employees than upper level employees, they make up the greatest percentage of the number of employees on the top two levels. Therefore, the correlation between the total number of employees and a part of the total should be high since there is approximately 80% of the total number of upper level employees are on the 2nd level rather than the first.

There were some correlations that dealt with financial stability that had high values and are shown in Table 5.

Table 5

Correlations Within Financial Data

Demographic Factor	Demographic Factor	Correlation
Yearly Sales	D&B Rating	0.34
Yearly Sales	Financial Stability	0.81
D&B Rating	Financial Stability	0.81

The reason for the high correlations between the financial stability rating and the yearly sales and the financial stability rating and Dun & Bradstreet rating is that the yearly sales multiplied by the Dun & Bradstreet rating is the financial stability rating, therefore, there would be a high correlation between the whole and its parts.

A final set of correlational analyses were performed between the demographic data and the POC factors, Leadership, Motivation, Communication, Goals, Decision and Control. Of the 96 different correlations, only six correlations showed a relationship with a correlation value of 0.30 or greater, and these were the averages of the various factors with Factor 26, which was the response average for all factors. This would be of note only if the correlations were not significant since there should be high correlations between the various parts and an average of those parts.

A majority of the correlations between the POC sub-factors, Factor 26 (the overall response average) and the demographic data were less than 0.30. In each case where the correlation was less than 0.30, indicating a relatively weak association, the relationships were not examined any further.

RESULTS OF HYPOTHESIS I

The higher the educational level of the organization's managers is, the more likely they are to use a participative management style of management. The operational hypothesis for this can be stated symbolically as,

$$H: p \neq 0 \ (\alpha = 0.05).$$

The null hypothesis for this can be stated symbolically as,

$$H_o: p = 0 \ (\alpha = 0.05),$$

where p is the population value of the correlation coefficient between the variables of educational level of the managers and the type of management style used.

The results of the correlation between the educational level of the managers and the likelihood of using participative management is 0.063. Testing the hypothesis using Student's t distribution, we obtain the following result,

$$t = 0.063 \sqrt{(162\text{-}2)/(1\text{-}(0.0040)^2} = 0.798$$

The critical values for t for $\alpha = 0.05$ is ± 1.97. Since the test statistic of 0.798 is found within the limits of the critical value, the null hypothesis is not rejected. The confidence interval was (-1.97, 1.97).

Since the critical value for the correlation coefficient is ± 0.156 ($\alpha = 0.05$) and the correlation is 0.063, the null hypothesis, that the correlation would be zero, is again, not rejected.

The interpretation of this is that no conclusion can be drawn as to whether or not there is a relationship between the educational level of the managers and whether or not the organization uses a participative form of management.

RESULTS OF HYPOTHESIS II

The older an organization is, the less likely it is to use a participative style of management. The operational hypothesis for this can be stated symbolically as,

$$H: p \neq 0 \ (\alpha = 0.05).$$

The null hypothesis for this can be stated symbolically as,

$$H_o: p = 0 \ (\alpha = 0.05)$$

where p is the population value of the correlation coefficient between the variables of the age of the organization and the type of management style used.

The results of the correlation between the age of the organization and the likelihood of using participative management is 0.018. Testing the hypothesis using Student's t distribution, we obtain the following result,

$$t = 0.018 \sqrt{(162\text{-}2)/(1\text{-}(0.0.0003)^2} = 0.228$$

The critical values for t for $\alpha = 0.05$ is ± 1.98. Since the test statistic of 0.2.28 is found within the limits of the confidence interval, the null hypothesis is not rejected. The confidence interval was (-1.98, 1.98).

Since the critical value for the correlation coefficient is approximately ± 0.156 ($\alpha = 0.05$) and the correlation is 0.018, the null hypothesis, that the correlation would be zero, is again, not rejected.

The interpretation of this is that no conclusion can be drawn as to whether or not there is a relationship between the age of an organization and whether or not the organization uses a participative form of management.

RESULTS OF HYPOTHESIS III

The older the organization's managers are, the less likely they are to use a participative style of management. The operational hypothesis for this can be stated symbolically as,

$$H: p \neq 0 \ (\alpha = 0.05).$$

The null hypothesis for this can be stated symbolically as,

$$H_o: p = 0 \ (\alpha = 0.05)$$

where p is the population value of the correlation coefficient between the variables of the age of the organization's managers and the type of management style used.

The results of the correlation between the age of the organization's managers and the likelihood of using participative management is 0.104. Testing the hypothesis using Student's t distribution, we obtain the following result,

$$t = 0.104\sqrt{(162-2)/(1-(0.0.0108)^2} = 1.323$$

The critical values for t for $\alpha = 0.05$ is ±1.98. Since the test statistic of 0.228 is found within the limits of the confidence interval, the null hypothesis is not rejected. The confidence interval was (-1.98, 1.98).

The critical value for the correlation coefficient is approximately ± 0.156 ($\alpha = 0.05$) and the correlation is 0.018, the null hypothesis, that the correlation would be zero, is again not rejected.

The interpretation of this is that no conclusion can be drawn as to whether or not there is a relationship between the age of an organization and whether or not the organization uses a participative form of management.

RESULTS OF HYPOTHESIS IV

Organizations who use a participative style of management are more likely to be smaller in size than organizations who use a more rigid style of management. The operational hypothesis for this can be stated symbolically as,

$$H: p \neq 0 \ (\alpha = 0.05).$$

The null hypothesis for this can be symbolically stated as

$$H_o: p = 0 \ (\alpha = 0.05)$$

where p is the population value of the correlation coefficient between the variables of size of the organization and the type of management style used.

The results of the correlation between the size of the organization and the likelihood of using participative management is 0.161. Testing the hypothesis using Student's t distribution, we obtain the following result,

$$t = 0.161\sqrt{(162-2)/(1-(0.0259)^2} = 2.063$$

The critical values for t for $\alpha = 0.05$ is ±1.98. Since the test statistic of 2.063 is not found within the limits of the critical value, the null hypothesis is rejected. The confidence interval was (-1.98, 1.98).

The critical value for the correlation coefficient is approximately ± 0.156 ($\alpha = 0.05$) and since the correlation is 0.161, the null hypothesis, that the correlation would be zero, is rejected.

The interpretation of this is that there is a relationship between the size of the organization and whether or not the organization uses a participative form of management. Interestingly, although the null hypothesis was rejected, the direction of the correlation was positive while the initial hypothesis would have yielded a negative correlation, had it been true, between the size of the organization and use of participative management. It appears therefore, that the size of the organization does make a difference in whether or not it uses a participative form of management, but participative management appears to be used more in larger rather than smaller organizations.

RESULTS OF HYPOTHESIS V

Organizations that use a participative style of management will have increased productivity that will result in increased financial stability. The operational hypothesis for this can be stated symbolically as,

$$H: p \neq 0 \ (\alpha = 0.05).$$

The null hypothesis for this can be symbolically stated as

$$H_o: p = 0 \ (\alpha = 0.05)$$

where p is the population value of the correlation coefficient between the variables of increased productivity, as defined by increased financial stability and the type of management style used.

The results of the correlation between the financial stability of the organization and the use of a participative style of management is 0.138. Testing the hypothesis using Student's t distribution, we obtain the following result,

$$t = 0.138 \sqrt{(96-2)/(1-(0.0190)^2} = 1.351$$

The critical values for t for $\alpha = 0.05$ is ± 1.98, which yields a confidence interval of (-1.98, 1.98). Since the test statistic of 1.351 is found within the limits of the critical value, the null hypothesis is not rejected.

The critical value for the correlation coefficient is approximately ±0.156 (α = 0.05) and since the correlation is 0.138, the null hypothesis, that the correlation would be zero, is again, not rejected.

The interpretation of this is that no conclusion can be drawn as to whether or not there is a relationship between the financial stability of an organization and whether or not the organization uses a participative form of management.

SUMMARY

162 surveys were received back out of 677 sent, or a return rate of 24%, and 91 of the responses came from companies where financial data was available, or 13.4% of the total surveys sent out. 9.9% of the 91 respondents were female with an average age of 41-46 with an average educational level of 3-4 years of college, while their male counterparts were 46-50 years old with just over 4 years of college.

A closer examination of the difference between the average response given by females and males revealed that females who worked in an organization where there was a female in the top executive position rated the management style very similar to their male colleagues whereas females who worked in organizations where a male held the top executive position rated the organization's style of management as being much more restrictive than their male colleagues.

An correlational analysis between the POC sub-factors with the average response of the POC (an average of all of the sub-factors) showed correlations of 0.63 to 0.79. An additional analysis was performed between the various factors of the POC, Leadership, Motivation, Communication, Goals, Decision and Control. These correlations ranged from 0.60 to 0.73.

A correlational analysis was executed on the demographic information and it was found that there were a number of correlations within the collected information that showed a definite relationship between the variables. Most of these related variables were concerned with the size, age and financial stability of the organization. The financial correlations, dealing with yearly sales and Dun & Bradstreet ratings, ranged from 0.34 to 0.81.

No support was shown for Hypotheses I, II, III and V, that is, this study showed no discernible relationship between:

1.   The educational level of the organizations's managers and the likelihood of using a participative style of management.

2.   The age of an organization and the likelihood of using a participative style of management.

3.   The age of the managers and the likelihood of using a participative style of management.

5.   Whether using a participative style of management causes an increase in financial stability.

The fourth hypothesis, "Organizations who use a participative style of management are more likely to be smaller in size than organizations who use a rigid style of management" did show a positive relationship.   Unfortunately, though, in order to fulfill the requirements of the hypothesis, the result should have been negative correlation, that is, the smaller organizations should have been more likely to use a participative style of management.   A positive correlation means that the larger an organization is, the more likely it is to use a participative style of management, the exact opposite of what was proposed in Hypothesis IV.

V

CONCLUSIONS AND RECOMMENDATIONS

CONCLUSIONS

Optimal productivity is the goal of every "for-profit" organization. Optimal productivity can be gained through the use of a number of different elements, including technologically advanced machinery, increased computer usage, redesigning work station flow and advanced management methods, to name a few.

One of the "new" management techniques is participative management, where everyone in the organization has some input into the decisions made. The advantages of participative management are obvious, you get input not only from the management side, but also from the workers, the employees who will be performing the work. This group of people know the actual production operation inside and out and are able to give additional insight that may not be readily apparent from casual observation.

Participative management also has problems, especially in its inception. Most managers in established organizations tend to continue running the organization as it had been run, following the axiom "If it ain't broke, don't fix it". Some of these managers are not easily able to relinquish the control that they have, and participative management requires that everyone share the responsibilities and decisions, although not necessarily on the same level.

Adherents of participative management strongly support the concept being applied to all organizations and at all levels, while its detractors point to the fact that no one is in clear control and making all of the decisions. Both viewpoints have flaws in how they portray their point of view and that of their opponents.

The review of literature examined a number of organizations, both private and public non-profit and "for profit" organizations, and their attempt to integrate some, if not all, of the elements of participative management into their organization's management structure. The general consensus of the studies was that participative styles of management help increase the efficiency of the organization, although actual "pre" and "post" implementation measurements of efficiency were not performed, therefore the most that can be said is that the use of participative management leads to better working conditions, in the opinion of the employees of the organizations about whom the articles were written.

Response Rate

The low response rate occurred for a number of different reasons that were listed earlier. The most likely reason that the surveys were not completed was that there was no "buy in" for the participants. It did not directly affect them since they were not involved other than filling out a questionnaire, it therefore gave little or no value for the time involved. Future studies of this nature might fare better if concentration were focused on a smaller number of companies, and these companies were visited in person. This would cause a face to be attached to the questionnaire which would allow the respondent to feel as though they were a bigger part of the project rather than just a set of numbers for another "college study".

Correlational Analyses

As stated previously, the correlations did not reveal any startling facts nor do they lead to any startling conclusions. There were a number of high correlations, however, since most of these correlations were measuring the same property, it would therefore stand to reason that they would correlate fairly well with themselves or similar factors. The correlations between sex and number of employees in the organization (0.18) and sex and the respondent's level in the organization (0.27) were calculated using a point bi-serial correlation because sex only has two conditions, female or male.

The correlations between number of employees and the number of work sites (0.59), the number of employees and number of employees on the respondent's level (0.35), the number of employees and number of employees in the top two levels of the company (0.46), the number of employees and annual sales ((0.73), number of employees and financial stability rating (0.61) are obviously going to be high due to the fact that Factor (Question) 17 asks for the total number of employees in the company. Each of the factors that correlate highly with Factor 17 (the number of employees) are concerned in some way with size of the organization or the logical results that occur as an organization increases in size. As an organization grows larger, there is an increase in the number of buildings occupied (Factor 18), more managers (Factors 21 and 22) to run the organization and the larger the organization the greater the annual sales (Factor 27). The financial stability rating (Factor 29) is a direct product of the annual sales (Factor 27) and the organization's current financial status, as appraised by Dun & Bradstreet (Factor 28), so if the correlation between the number of employees and annual sales is high, then the correlation between the number of employees and the financial stability rating will also be high.

The correlations between the number of work sites and annual sales (0.44), the number of work sites and the financial stability rating (0.39) are high due primarily to the same reasons that the correlations involving the number of employees are high, larger organizations have larger infrastructures.

The correlations involving the organization's age and financial stability rating (0.41)) are also significant for the same reasons that were stated earlier in the analysis of factors involving the number of employees and the number of work sites, that is, as organizations grow older, they usually get larger, with more employees and more work sites.

The high correlation between number of employees on the respondent's level and number of employees on the top two levels of management (0.79) is clearly due to the fact that they are both measuring the number of members in each of the two top levels of the organization. Obviously, there will always be either the same or more total employees in the top two levels of the organization than there will be in either of the component levels (the sum is equal to the total of its parts).

The correlation between the number of employees on respondent's level and the yearly sales (0.32) is easily explained by the fact that companies with greater sales volumes are usually larger companies and have more top level managers.

The final correlations examined were between the yearly sales and the Dun & Bradstreet rating) (0.34), the yearly sales and the financial stability rating (0.81), and the Dun & Bradstreet rating and the financial stability rating (0.81). Basically, the correlation between the yearly sales and the Dun & Bradstreet rating shows that the companies who have greater sales volumes are more likely to be financially secure. This again is a fairly obvious and logical observation. The correlations between the financial stability rating and the yearly sales and the Dun & Bradstreet rating are high due to the fact that the financial stability rating is the product of the numerical values of the annual sales and the Dun & Bradstreet rating, therefore there would be a direct, positive relationship between the size or size increase in either of those factors and an increase in the final product.

The correlations between the various parts of the POC correlate rather highly with themselves, that is, each of the different subsections of the POC are highly correlated with the other subsections. Although these high correlations have little bearing on the hypotheses examined in this study, it is important to note because if the subsections did not correlate well, the entire instrument would be suspect as a valid measure of management styles.

There were *t* tests performed on the averages of the responses based on sex of the respondent, to determine whether or not the response mean of the females could be part of the sample mean. The first *t* test was performed to see whether or not the response averages from females were could be contained within the sample averages. The null hypothesis (that there was no difference between female and male response averages) was not rejected , so the females responses were split into two different averages, those with a female in a Level 1 position and those without a female in a Level 1 position. It was found that those females with a female in a Level 1 position had an average that was slightly higher than the overall population average. It was also found, though, that females in organizations where there was not a Level 1 female had response averages that were well outside critical limits. In other words, females in organizations where there were no upper level management females did not see the organization's style of management in the same light as their male counterparts in the same organization.

This could be interpreted in any number of different ways, but the most likely interpretation is that there is sexual bias within the organizations polled. Females who were Level 2 employees within an organization where there was a Level 1 female employee gave the highest responses for females to the questionnaire. At the same time, Level 2 females within organizations with Level 1 males were more likely to give responses lower than their male colleagues to the POC.

Hypotheses

Four out of five hypotheses that were tested did not prove out, and the one that did actually resulted in the opposite conclusion from what was originally stated. There are a number of reasons that this could have occurred that the hypotheses could have failed. The possible reasons will be discussed for each hypothesis.

Hypothesis I

The higher the educational level of the organization's management is, the more likely it is to use a participative style of management.

The basic assumption that was made when this hypothesis was developed was that participative management techniques are discussed and taught in upper level college courses, therefore, it is logical to expect that the more higher education a person has pursued, the more likely it is that they would have been exposed to the concepts of participative management. One of the most obvious fallacies of this logic is that participative management has become a very common topic in numerous magazines and in many "mini" seminars around the country. Management experts often point to the Japanese, as models for consensus building, as an example of participative management at work.

It no longer, therefore, is the case that it is necessary for a person to take higher level college courses in order to learn about participative management.

Hypothesis II

The older an organization is, the less likely it is to use a participative style of management. The underlying assumption here was, again, that in order to learn about participative management, it would be necessary to take advanced level college courses. Older managers would have taken advanced college level courses when the theory of participative management was considered to be a "pipe dream" and something of little or no consequence. Once again, the surprising dominance of the Japanese in the world marketplace caused the concepts of participative management to be re-considered in a different light, spawning an avid desire to know what the Japanese knew and what we did not.

Hypothesis III

The older an organization's managers are, the less likely they are to use a participative style of management. The basic management philosophies taught in the from the early 1900's until the early to mid 1980's were based on Frederick Taylor and the other early industrial engineers. These philosophies stressed a "one-man" operation, run from the top down, just like a military unit is run. The primary job of top management was to make decisions and pass them down to the middle management for implementation. The middle managers were responsible to oversee the actual operations and the job of the shop or floor employees was to perform the work. Good ideas were encouraged from the ranks primarily through monetary incentives and company recognition. The original conjecture that formed the base of Hypothesis II was that the older the managers were, the more likely it was that the fundamental management style that they were taught was the "top down" model. A item to consider at this point is that the response average for the entire sample that was used was 5.39 out of a total scale that ranged from one to eight. This actually puts the response average in the consultative management style rather than in a true participative management style. It is, therefore, conceivable that although the null hypothesis was not rejected, that the "top down" model did and still does influence upper management behavior, resulting in a lower response average.

Hypothesis IV

Organizations who use a participative style of management are more likely to be smaller in size than organizations who use a rigid style of management. The null hypothesis was rejected, unfortunately, in order for the original hypothesis to be true, the resulting analyses would have to have been numerically negative, that is, if smaller organizations were indeed more likely to use a participative style of management than larger organizations, a numerical decrease in the size of the organization would have been accompanied by a numerical increase in the response average on the POC. Instead, the was a increase in the response average as the organizations grew larger.

There is no logical explanation for this phenomenon, especially since the number of large, small and medium organizations was equally distributed throughout the returned responses. At this time, the reason for this result is unknown. It is unclear whether this is an actual cause and effect relationship or just an anomaly.

Hypothesis V

Organizations that use a participative style of management will have increased productivity that will result in increased financial stability. In order to define what effects should be visible in organizations that use participative forms for management, a number of financial experts were consulted. The general consensus of the experts was that if an organization was performing efficiently, its financial stability and annual sales would be the first measurable items that would be affected. It was also decided to multiply the two items together, thus enhancing the effects of both good and bad performance by organizations. The biggest problem was that it appeared that all organizations were using similar styles of management, as evidenced by the homogeneity of the response averages for each organization.

RECOMMENDATIONS

The null hypotheses for Hypotheses I, II, III and V were not rejected. This does not necessarily mean that there is no effect, but rather that whatever effect that it had was not measurable against background noise. One of the problems is that the instrument is self-administered. This can cause several concerns, including whether or not the respondent thought or was apprehensive about the possibility of their answers be available to their superiors. Although the respondents were assured that their answers would remain anonymous, if the organization style leaned towards the exploitative or even the benevolent style of management, this could have caused anxiety about answering truthfully.

Another problem with self administered instruments is the fact of interpretation of what any particular phrase means. Some people will view an benevolent style of management as an enlightened way of doing business while others will view it as a return to the "sweat shops" of the early 1900s. This was seen many times in the results that were received, particularly in one case where two respondents of

the same sex, had very similar responses, indicating, by the pattern of
their answers, that the organization was definitely using the participative style of management. The third respondent from the same organization was of a different sex and from their perspective, the style was
just short of whips and chains, with a large number of negative responses.

Another problem may be that the tool used to measure financial
stability may not have been sensitive enough to measure actual differences in worth. Although the financial ratings of institutions such as
Dun & Bradstreet are used every day to make major, crucial decisions
in the business world, these indicators may not be discriminating
enough to help discern between the differences in a strong market
competitor who uses an exploitative style of management and a strong
market competitor who uses a more participative style of management.

It could also be that the tool was not measuring an appropriate co-
variant. As stated previously, one of the assumptions that was being
examined is that a participative style of management increases productivity and increased productivity results in an organization that has
increased financial stability. There are however, other factors that
can affect an organization's financial stability, including currency
exchange rates, interest rates, product diversification and so on. At
this point, it is doubtful that there is any financial co-variant that
could be used to measure the true effect of a participative style of
management on an organization's productivity.

Study Format Changes

In order to accurately gauge the effect of a participative style of
management and its effects on productivity, it will be necessary to
actually go into the organizations under study and take productivity
measurements, or obtain valid historical measurements that track
productivity over time with care taken to insure that other competing
variables are not influencing any productivity changes, such as the
introduction of gain sharing or profit sharing plans or the change from
a non-union to a union environment or the visa versa.

Since the null hypothesis of one of the hypotheses (Hypothesis
IV), "Organizations who use a participative style of management are
more likely to be smaller in size than organizations who use a more
rigid style of management", was rejected, then it can be inferred that

larger organizations are more likely to use a participative style of management. It would make any future study of this subject more valid if comparisons of style were performed on subject organizations that were closely matched on size and other physical characteristics. The only variable that would differ between the individual members of matched pairs would be their ratings on their style of management, with each organization have distinctly different styles of management.

Part of the study would also involve measurement of the management style, but do to the interfering factors that were mentioned earlier, it would be advantageous for the researcher to conduct all analyses of the management style rather than rely on self administration.

SUMMARY

Although the study did produce some interesting data and insights into the use of participative management in organizations, there were some flaws.

In order to correct the flaws in the study, it is recommended that for future studies, the analysis of the organization's style of management be performed by one person rather than relying on individuals within the organization to complete the questionnaire themselves.

The second recommendation would be to match organizations on the basis of their physical characteristics, that is, size, number of employees, annual sales, etc., and then assess their efficiency and what style of management they use.

The third and final recommendation is that the study use data from within each organization on actual efficiencies to determine whether or not a participative style of management would be conducive to increased efficiencies over other styles of management.

TABLE 1

DEMOGRAPHIC CHARACTERISTICS OF THE RESPONDENT SAMPLE

Factor	Female	Male	Average
Age of Respondent	41-45	46-50	46-50
Education	2.9	3.3	3.3
Level 1 Employee	6	65	71*
% Level 1	40.0%	44.2%	43.9%
Level 2 Employee	9	82	91*
% Level 2	60.0%	55.8%	56.2%
Response Average	4.83	5.44	5.39
Level I Females	5.68	- - -	- - -
Level II Females	4.32	- - -	- - -
# of Employees	151-250	500+	500+
# of Buildings	3	9	8
Age of Organization	31-40	36-45	36-45
Organizational Sales Average	$40MM	$65MM	$60MM

* Total

TABLE 2

COMPARISON BETWEEN POC SUB-FACTORS AND SUB-FACTOR AVERAGE (FACTOR 26)

Sub-Factor Number	Sub-Factor Type	Correlation
1	Leadership	0.75
2	Leadership	0.71
3	Leadership	0.71
4	Motivation	0.66
5	Motivation	0.66
6	Motivation	0.77
7	Communication	0.66
8	Communication	0.70
9	Communication	0.63
10	Communication	0.65
11	Decision	0.74
12	Decision	0.78
13	Goals	0.75
14	Goals	0.67
15	Control	0.69
16	Control	0.72

TABLE 3

CORRELATIONS BETWEEN POC FACTORS

POC Factor	POC Factor	Correlation
Leadership	Motivation	0.70
Leadership	Communication	0.63
Leadership	Decision	0.64
Leadership	Goals	0.63
Leadership	Control	0.65
Motivation	Communication	0.69
Motivation	Decision	0.62
Motivation	Goals	0.68
Motivation	Control	0.65
Communication	Decision	0.69
Communication	Goals	0.68
Communication	Control	0.61
Decision	Goals	0.73
Decision	Control	0.63
Goals	Control	0.60

TABLE 4

CORRELATIONS BETWEEN DEMOGRAPHIC
FACTORS EXCEEDING 0.29

Demographic Factor	Demographic Factor	Correlation
# of Employees	# of Work Sites	0.59
# of Employees	# of Employees on Respondent's Level	0.35
# of Employees	# of Employees on Top Two Levels	0.46
# of Employees	Annual Sales	0.73
# of Employees	Financial Stability	0.61
# of Sites	Annual Sales	0.44
# of Sites	Financial Stability	0.39
Organization's Age	Financial Stability	0.41
Respondent's Level	Respondent's Sex	0.30*
# of Employees on Respondent's Level	# of Employees on Top Two Levels	0.79
# of Employees on Respondent's Level	Financial Stability	0.41
# of Employees on Top Two Levels	Financial Stability	0.36

* Performed using a point bi-serial correlation

APPENDIX A
FACTOR/QUESTION LIST

Question	Definition
1	P.O.C. Leadership sub-factor
2	P.O.C. Leadership sub-factor
3	P.O.C. Leadership sub-factor
4	P.O.C. Motivation sub-factor
5	P.O.C. Motivation sub-factor
6	P.O.C. Motivation sub-factor
7	P.O.C. Communication sub-factor
8	P.O.C. Communication sub-factor
9	P.O.C. Communication sub-factor
10	P.O.C. Communication sub-factor
11	P.O.C. Decision sub-factor
12	P.O.C. Decision sub-factor
13	P.O.C. Goals sub-factor
14	P.O.C. Goals sub-factor
15	P.O.C. Control sub-factor
16	P.O.C. Control sub-factor
17	Number of employees in respondent's organization
18	Number of buildings in respondent's organization
19	Organization's age
20	Respondent's organizational level
21	Number of employees on respondent's level
22	Number of employees in top two management levels
23	Respondent's educational attainment level
24	Respondent's gender
25	Respondent's age
26	Average of responses to Questions 1-16
27	Annual sales from Dun & Bradstreet
28	Current financial status from Dun & Bradstreet
29	Financial stability rating

CORRELATION MATRIX OF POC SUB-SECTIONS WITH POC SUB-SECTIONS

	L2	L3	M1	M2	M3	CM1	CM2	CM3	CM4	D1	D2	G1	G2	CT1	CT2
L1	0.61	0.56	0.50	0.46	0.53	0.43	0.43	0.43	0.44	0.54	0.50	0.50	0.49	0.47	0.49
L2	–	0.62	0.46	0.33	0.57	0.33	0.43	0.40	0.51	0.45	0.52	0.51	0.35	0.48	0.52
L3	–	–	0.47	0.47	0.53	0.33	0.45	0.34	0.42	0.42	0.57	0.52	0.35	0.44	0.50
M1	–	–	–	0.30	0.48	0.41	0.38	0.39	0.33	0.35	0.44	0.51	0.32	0.39	0.55
M2	–	–	–	–	0.53	0.46	0.40	0.43	0.27	0.47	0.42	0.36	0.57	0.41	0.35
M3	–	–	–	–	–	0.49	0.47	0.47	0.50	0.51	0.54	0.48	0.51	0.49	0.57
CM1	–	–	–	–	–	–	0.48	0.40	0.31	0.48	0.42	0.49	0.47	0.47	0.36
CM2	–	–	–	–	–	–	–	0.43	0.49	0.47	0.51	0.42	0.49	0.36	0.44
CM3	–	–	–	–	–	–	–	–	0.49	0.45	0.48	0.41	0.40	0.80	0.34
CM4	–	–	–	–	–	–	–	–	–	0.46	0.58	0.43	0.38	0.39	0.48
D1	–	–	–	–	–	–	–	–	–	–	0.65	0.60	0.44	0.51	0.47
D2	–	–	–	–	–	–	–	–	–	–	–	0.71	0.50	0.51	0.53
G1	–	–	–	–	–	–	–	–	–	–	–	–	0.45	0.45	0.47
G2	–	–	–	–	–	–	–	–	–	–	–	–	–	0.40	0.46
CT1	–	–	–	–	–	–	–	–	–	–	–	–	–	–	0.53

L = LEADERSHIP
M = MOTIVATION
CM = COMMUNCATION
D = DECISION
G = GOALS
CT = CONTROL

APPENDIX C

CORRELATION MATRIX OF INDIVIDUAL POC FACTORS

	2	3	4	5	6	7	8	9	10	11	12	13	14	15	16	17	18	19	20	21	22	23	24	25	26	27	28	29
1	0.61	0.56	0.50	0.46	0.53	0.43	0.43	0.43	0.44	0.54	0.50	0.50	0.49	0.47	0.49	0.18	0.21	0.03	0.15	0.12	0.05	0.04	0.15	0.00	0.75	0.18	0.06	0.07
2		0.62	0.46	0.33	0.57	0.33	0.43	0.40	0.51	0.45	0.52	0.51	0.35	0.48	0.52	0.18	0.23	0.00	0.08	0.05	0.03	0.07	0.20	0.03	0.71	0.13	0.14	0.03
3			0.47	0.47	0.53	0.33	0.45	0.34	0.42	0.42	0.57	0.52	0.35	0.44	0.50	0.18	0.11	0.01	0.01	0.18	0.10	0.01	0.18	0.10	0.71	0.20	0.06	0.10
4				0.30	0.48	0.41	0.38	0.39	0.33	0.35	0.44	0.51	0.32	0.39	0.55	0.07	0.12	0.08	0.04	0.14	0.08	0.02	0.10	0.06	0.66	0.15	0.01	0.08
5					0.53	0.46	0.40	0.43	0.27	0.47	0.42	0.36	0.57	0.41	0.35	0.12	0.02	0.09	0.02	0.02	0.03	0.00	0.16	0.10	0.66	0.19	0.14	0.20
6						0.49	0.47	0.47	0.50	0.51	0.54	0.48	0.51	0.49	0.57	0.15	0.01	0.05	0.14	0.02	0.07	0.04	0.17	0.20	0.77	0.18	0.08	0.19
7							0.48	0.40	0.31	0.48	0.42	0.49	0.47	0.47	0.36	0.15	0.01	0.01	0.06	0.01	0.09	0.09	0.11	0.07	0.66	0.06	0.03	0.01
8								0.43	0.49	0.47	0.51	0.42	0.49	0.36	0.44	0.03	0.08	0.13	0.08	0.06	0.01	0.07	0.04	0.11	0.07	0.06	0.02	0.00
9									0.49	0.45	0.48	0.41	0.40	0.38	0.34	0.02	0.20	0.03	0.09	0.01	0.05	0.01	0.10	0.02	0.63	0.10	0.11	0.03
10										0.46	0.58	0.43	0.38	0.39	0.48	0.14	0.04	0.12	0.06	0.04	0.01	0.12	0.20	0.09	0.65	0.01	0.05	0.05
11											0.65	0.60	0.44	0.51	0.47	0.51	0.19	0.05	0.05	0.11	0.01	0.17	0.16	0.07	0.74	0.19	0.00	0.12
12												0.71	0.50	0.51	0.53	0.16	0.14	0.02	0.03	0.08	0.04	0.08	0.22	0.15	0.78	0.21	0.01	0.15
13													0.45	0.45	0.47	0.14	0.16	0.00	0.05	0.08	0.01	0.08	0.23	0.05	0.75	0.18	0.03	0.07
14														0.40	0.46	0.17	0.11	0.14	0.07	0.05	0.12	0.05	0.08	0.16	0.67	0.24	0.06	0.15
15															0.53	0.23	0.05	0.10	0.12	0.07	0.05	0.03	0.24	0.06	0.69	0.17	0.11	0.17
16																0.06	0.06	0.09	0.00	0.12	0.02	0.21	0.10	0.12	0.72	0.17	0.12	0.15
17																	0.59	0.28	0.02	0.35	0.46	0.16	0.17	0.15	0.16	0.73	0.14	0.61
18																		0.04	0.00	0.11	0.19	0.03	0.11	0.05	0.16	0.44	0.09	0.39
19																			0.04	0.26	0.30	0.12	0.07	0.05	0.02	0.19	0.25	0.41
20																				0.26	0.04	0.05	0.30	0.25	0.09	0.01	0.02	0.01
21																					0.79	0.17	0.12	0.00	0.08	0.28	0.25	0.41
22																						0.17	0.02	0.06	0.08	0.32	0.16	0.36
23																							0.03	0.09	0.06	0.24	0.06	0.19
24																								0.12	0.22	0.22	0.08	0.12
25																									0.10	0.17	0.13	0.16
26																										0.22	0.01	0.14
27																											0.34	0.81
28																												0.81

APPENDIX D

FEMALE - MALE RESPONSE ANALYSES

Factor	Female	Male	Overall
Age	41-50	46-55	46-55
Education	2.9	3.3	3.3
Level 1 Employees	6	65	71
% Level 1	40.0%	44.2%	43.9%
Level 2 Employees	9	82	91
% Level 2	60.0%	55.8%	56.2%
# of Employees	151-250	500+	500+
# of Buildings	3	9	8
Response Average	4.83	5.44	5.39
Sales Average	6.80	8.38	8.23

APPENDIX E

This survey was developed to help people describe the type of management style their organization uses. It is important to remember that there is no right or wrong answer, so please answer each question the best you can. The answers that you give will be kept totally confidential.

Each question can be answered using an 8 point scale, as illustrated below:

Seldom		Occasionally		Frequently		Almost Always	
1	2	3	4	5	6	7	8

If the question asks whether or not you feel that work is rewarded promptly and you felt that the answer was not "Almost Always", but more than "Occasionally", then you would circle either 5 or 6, whichever number you felt was closer to what you feel the answer is.

Please be sure to complete questions, place the questionnaire into the self-addressed, stamped envelope and mail when you are finished.

This survey takes no more than 5-7 minutes to complete. Thank you for your cooperation. An abstract of the study will be sent to all parties that respond, and copies of the final results and an executive summary may be obtained by writing to:

Michael H. Swearingen
C/O Dr. U. Smidchens
Western Michigan University
Dept. of Educational Leadership
Kalamazoo, MI 49002

LEADERSHIP

1. How much confidence and trust is shown in subordinates?

Very little		Some		Quite a bit		A very great deal	
1	2	3	4	5	6	7	8

2. How free do subordinates feel to talk to superiors about their work?

Not free		Somewhat free		Quite free		Very free	
1	2	3	4	5	6	7	8

3. How often are subordinates' ideas sought and used constructively?

Seldom		Occasionally		Frequently		Almost Always	
1	2	3	4	5	6	7	8

MOTIVATION

4. Is predominant use made of: a) fear, b) threats, c) punishment, d) rewards, e) involvement?

a,b,c and occasionally d		d with some c		Mainly d with some c and e		d and e, based on group set goals	
1	2	3	4	5	6	7	8

5. Where is responsibility felt for achieving high performance?

Mostly at top		Top and middle		Fairly widespread		At all levels	
1	2	3	4	5	6	7	8

6. How much cooperative teamwork exists?

Very little		Some		Quite a bit		A great deal	
1	2	3	4	5	6	7	8

COMMUNICATION

7. What is the usual direction of information flow?

Top down		Mostly down		Up & down		Up, down and sideways	
1	2	3	4	5	6	7	8

8. How is downward communication accepted?

With distrust		Often with suspicion		Often accepted		Fully Accepted	
1	2	3	4	5	6	7	8

9. How accurate is upward communication?

Usually Inaccurate		Occasionally Inaccurate		Often Accurate		Almost always Accurate	
1	2	3	4	5	6	7	8

10. How well do superiors know the problems faced by subordinates?

Not well		Somewhat		Quite well		Very well	
1	2	3	4	5	6	7	8

DECISIONS

11. At what level are decisions made?

Mostly at top		Policy at top, some delegation		General policy at top, more delegation		Widespread decision making, well coordinated	
1	2	3	4	5	6	7	8

12. How often are subordinates involved in decisions related to their work?

	Occasionally Consulted		Generally Consulted		Fully Involved	
Almost never						
1	2	3	4	5	6	7	8

GOALS

13. How is goal setting usually done?

Orders issued	Orders, some comments		By orders after discussion		Generally by group discussion	
1	2	3	4	5	6	7	8

14. How much do subordinates strive to achieve organization's goals?

Very little		Some		Quite a bit		A great deal	
1	2	3	4	5	6	7	8

CONTROL

15. How concentrated are review and control functions?

Very highly at top		Highly at top		Moderate delegation at lower levels		Widely Shared	
1	2	3	4	5	6	7	8

16. What are cost, productivity, and other control data used for?

Policing, punishment		Reward and punishment		Reward, some self-guidance		Group guidance & problem solving	
1	2	3	4	5	6	7	8

DEMOGRAPHIC DATA

17. Total number of full time employees? 1-25 ___ 26-75 ___
    76-150 ___ 151-250 ___ 251-500 ___ 501-1000 ___
    1001-2000 ___ 2001-5000 ___ 5001-10,000 ___ 10,001 + ___

18. Total number of employee work sites (separate buildings). _____

19. Number of years in business? 0-2___ 3-5___ 6-8___ 9-12___
    13-16___ 17-20___ 21-25___ 26-30___ 31-35___ 36-40___
    41-45___ 46-50___ 51-60___ 61-75___ 76-100___ 101+___

20. Your level in your organization.
    a.   1st (CEO, president, plant manager, director, etc.) ___
    b.   2nd echelon (vice president, section manager, etc.) ___

21. How many persons are there on your level? _____

22. How many persons are there in the top two levels of your organization? _____

23. Your educational level. High school ___ Associate's degree or some college ___ 4 year degree ___ Graduate degree ___ Specialist degree ___ Doctoral degree ___ M.D., O.D., D.V.M., etc. ___

24. Your sex. Female ___ Male ___

25. Your age. 18-25___ 26-30___ 31-35___ 36-40___ 41-45___ 46-50___ 51-55___ 55-60___ 61-65___ 66+___

Thank you for the time you spent in filling out this survey.

APPENDIX F

CORRELATION MATRIX OF POC CATEGORIES

	M	C1	D	G	C2
L	0.70	0.63	0.64	0.63	0.65
M	----	0.69	0.62	0.68	0.65
C1	----	----	0.69	0.68	0.61
D	----	----	----	0.73	0.63
G	----	----	----	----	0.60

L = Leadership

M = Motivation

C1 = Communication

D = Decisions

G = Goals

C2 = Control

Bibliography

Anard, K. N. (1995). *Which Comes First: The Chicken or The Egg?*. Quality Progress, May, 1995, p.115-118.

Anderson, M. E. (1988). *The Management Team. Patterns for Success*. Eugene, OR: University of Oregon School Study Council.

Balch, D. E. & Blanck, R. (1989). *Measuring The Quality of Work Life*. Quality Progress, November, 1989, p. 44-48.

Barnhard, N. (1980). *Human Factors in Library Administration*. Medical Library Association (Courses for Continuing Education), Chicago, IL.

Beehr, T. A. & Gupta, N. (1982). *Managerial Styles and Employee Responses*. Paper presented at the Annual Meeting of The Midwestern Psychological Association (54th), Minneapolis, MN.

Bertrand, W. S. (1992). *Designing Quality Into Work Life*. Quality Progress, June, 1992, p. 29-33.

Bradford, D. L. & Cohen, A. R. (1984). *Managing for Excellence: The Guide to Developing High Performance in Contemporary Organizations*. New York: John Wiley & Sons.

Branst, L. & Dubberly, A. (1988). *Labor/Management Participation: The NUMMI Experience*. Quality Progress, April, 1988, p.30-34.

Bruner, J. S. (1957). *On Going Beyond The Information Given Presented*. Contemporary Approaches to Cognition. Cambridge, MA: Harvard University Press.

Collins, D. (1995). *Death of a Gainsharing Plan: Power Politics and Participatory Management.*. Organizational Dynamics, Summer, 1995, V.24, p. 23.

Doucouliagos, C. (1993). *Worker Participation in Labor Managed and Participatory Capitalist Firms: a Meta-Analysis.* Industrial and Labor Relations, October, 1995, p. 37-75.

Drewes, D. W. (1982). *Working for America: a Work-Centered Approach to Productivity Improvement.* Viewpoints. (Available from Conserva, Inc., 401 Oberlin Road, Raleigh, NC 27605).

Dun & Bradstreet. (1991). *1991 Million Dollar Directory series.* Bethlehem, PA: Author.

Elvins, J. P. (1985). *Communication in Quality Circles: Members' Perceptions of Their Participation and its Effects on Related Organizational Communication Variables.* Paper presented at the Annual Meeting of the International Communication Association (35th), Honolulu, HI.

Feldman, J. M. (1993). *In Europe, Work Councils: Employee Participation on Company Boards in The Norm but The Need for Cost Cutting is Altering The Landscape.* Air Transport World, February, 1993, p. 56-59.

Fish, M. & Adams, R.C. (1985, November). *Personnel Characteristics, Job Satisfaction, and Organizational Styles of Television Program Directors Over Market Ranks and Station Sizes.* Paper presented at the Annual Meeting of the Speech Communication Association (71st), Denver, CO.

Flood, D. E. (1985). *I am a Leader! The Idiots Won't Follow!* Paper presented at the Annual Meeting of the National Association of Elementary School principals.

Frost, C. F., Wakely, J. H., & Ruh, R. A. (1974). *The Scanlon Plan for Organization Development: Identity, Participation, and Equity.* Lansing, MI: Michigan State University Press.

Games, P. A. & Klare, G. E. (1967). *Elementary Statistics - Data Analysis for The Behavioral Sciences.* New York: McGraw-Hill Book Company.

Gaziano, C. & Coulson, D. C. (1987). *Effect of Newsroom Management Styles on Journalists: a Case Study of Two Newspapers.* Paper presented at the Annual Meeting of the Association for Education in Journalism and Mass Communication (70th), San Antonio, TX.

Glaser, E. M. (1973). *Improving The Quality of Worklife,...and in The Process, Improving Productivity: a Summary of Concepts, Procedures and Problems, with Case Histories.* Los Angles, CA: Human Interaction Research Institute.

Greeno, J. G. (1978). *A Study of Problem Solving.* In R. Glaser (ed.) Instructional Psychology. Hillsdale, NJ: Lawrence Erlbaum Associates.

Harley, R.T. (1993). *The Truth About American Workers.* Industry Week, May 3, 1993, Vol. 242, p. 75.

Harris, T. E. (1986). *Organizational Communication: Focusing on Leadership Behaviors and Change Management.* Paper presented at the Annual Meeting of the Speech Association (72nd), Chicago, IL.

Harris, T. E. (1987). *Leading and Managing: a Study of Style and Perception.* Paper presented at the Annual Meeting of Western Speech Communication Association, Salt Lake City, UT.

Hellweg, S. A. & Freiberg, K. L. (1984). *Corporate Quality Circles: Theoretical and Pragmatic Extensions.* Paper presented at the Annual Meeting of the International Communication Association (34th), San Francisco, CA.

Heppner, P. P. (1978). *A Review of Problem Solving Literature and its Relationship to The Counseling Process.* Journal of Counseling Psychology, 25, No. 5, 366-375.

Hinkle, D. E., Wiersma, W. & Jurs, S. G. (1988). *Applied Statistics for The Behavioral Sciences.* Boston: Houghton Mifflin Company.

Hopkins, K. D. & Glass, G. V. (1978). *Basic Statistics for The Behavioral Sciences*. Englewood Cliffs, NJ: Prentice-Hall Inc.

Huitema, B. E. (1980). *The Analysis of Covariance and Alternatives*. New York: John Wiley & Sons, Inc.

Isenhart, M. W. (1986). *Participative Management in a Theological Institution*. Paper presented at the Annual Meeting of the Speech Association (72nd), Chicago, IL.

Kerlinger, F. N. (1986). *Foundations of Behavioral Research*. New York: Holt, Rinehart and Winston.

Ketchel, J. M. (1972). *Comparison of Effectiveness of Public Health Offices and Management Styles Using The Profile of Organizational Characteristics*. Published doctoral dissertation, Institute for Social Research, University of Michigan.

Lawler, E. E. III (1982). *Education, Management Style, and Organizational Effectiveness*. National Institute of Education, Washington, DC.

Likert, R. A. (1967). *The Human Organization: its Management and Value*. New York: McGraw.

Likert, R. A. & Likert, J. G. (1976). *New Ways of Managing Conflict*. New York: McGraw.

Lloyd, R. F. & Rehg, V. R. (1983). *Quality Circles: Applications in Vocational Education*. Information Series No. 249, Columbus, OH: Ohio State University National Center for Vocational Education.

McCabe, D. M. (1984). *The Labor-Management Communication Process: Current Developments in Labor-Management Cooperation*. Proceedings of the American Business Communication Association Southwest Convention (31st) (pp 193-198), Hammond, LA.

McGrath, T. C. (1993). *Gainsharing: Engineering The Human Factor of Productivity.* Industrial Engineering, September, 1993,p. 61-62.

Milutinovich, J. S., Gluskinos, U. M., & Viola, R. H. (1971). *A Stepwise Discriminat Analysis of Job Satisfaction and Group Cohesiveness of Biracial Blue and White Collar Workers.* Paper presented at the Annual Meeting of the Eastern Psychological Association (42nd), New York, NY.

Moeser, E. L. & Golen, L. L. (1987). *Participative Management: a Labor Management Process That Works for Kids.* Paper presented at the Annual Meeting of the National School Boards Association, San Francisco, CA.

Moore, B. E. & Ross, T. L. (1987). *The Scanlon Way to Improved Productivity: a Practical Guide.* New York, NY: John Wiley & Sons, Inc.

Moretz, H. L. (1983). *Quality Circles: Involvement, Problem-Solving, and Recognition.* Innovative Abstracts, 5, No. 12, 1-2.

Nash, D. A. (1985). *A Profile of Organizational Characteristics of Colleges of Dentistry.* Journal of Dental Education, 49, No. 3, 140-144.

New Mexico Research and Study Council. (1983). *Increasing Personal and Organizational Effectiveness.* (Treatise No. 3).

Nilsson, W. P. (1984). *Management Development at Hewlett-Packard.* Making Our Schools More Effective: Proceedings of Three State Conferences (pp 241-248). Washington, D.C.: U.S. Department of Education.

Ollins, S. K. (1990). *Opportunity Assessment and Planning Process Works for EG&G's Group Problem Solving.* Industrial Engineering, June, 1990, p 40-45.

Owens, R. G. (1987). *Organizational Behavior in Education.* Englewood Cliffs, NJ: Prentice-Hall.

Pejovich, S. (1984). *Industrial Democracy: Conflict or Cooperation?*
Series on Public Issues N0.12, College Station, TX: Texas A&M
University Center for Free Enterprise.

Phillips, D. D. (1977). *A Systematic Study of Communication at The
Corporate Level of Two Television Group Owners*. Paper present-
ed at the Annual Meeting of Western Speech Communication
Association, Phoenix, AZ.

Pratzner, F. C. & Russell, J. F. (1984). *The Changing Workplace:
Implications of Quality of Work Life Developments for Vocational
Education*. Research and Development Series No. 249, Colum-
bus, OH: Ohio State University National Center for Vocational
Education.

Robinson, N. (1985). *Productivity: an Overview*. Connecticut State
Department of Education, Bureau of Vocational Technical
Schools, Hartford, CT.

Rouda, R. H. (1995). *Development of Human Resources: Part 5:
Managing Change With Large Scale, Real Time Interventions*.
Tappi Journal, December, 1995, p. 240-242.

Ryan, J. (1988). *Labor/Management Participation: The A. O. Smith
Experience*. Quality Progress, April, 1988, p. 36-40.

Satterwhite, F. J. O. (1982). *Managing Quality Circles Effectively*.
Educational Quality Circle Consortium Monograph, Redwood,
CA: San Mateo County Office of Education.

Savage, G. T. (1984). *Decision Making as Negotiation: a Comparison
of Two Labor Management Committees*. Paper presented at the
Annual Meeting of the International Communication Association
(34th), San Francisco, CA.

Savage, R. T. & Romano, R. (1983). *Equality in the Workplace:
Quality Circles or Quality of Working Life Programs in The US*.
Paper presented at the Annual Meeting of the Eastern Communi-
cation Association, Ocean City, MD.

Schaeffer, C. (1996). *Performance Measurement Drives Enterprise Integration.* IIE Solutions, March, 1996, p. 20-27.

Schmerl, H. (1989). *Port Authority Improves Productivity Through PMP.* Public Works, May, 1989, p. 70-72.

Schuster, M. H. (1982). *Union-Management Cooperation, Structure, Process and Impact.* W.E. Upjohn Institute of Employment Research, Kalamazoo, MI.

Semlak, W. D., Cragan, J. & Cuffe, M. (1986, April). *Corporate Culture in a University Setting: an Analysis of Theory "X", Theory "Y", and Theory "Z" Cultures Within Departments.* Paper presented at the Annual Meeting of the Central States Speech Association, Cincinnati, OH.

Small, S. E. (1987). *Educational Needs and Wants: Identification and Acquisition Through Participative Management Structures. Quality circles.* Paper presented at the Annual Conference of the National Council of States of Inservice Education (12th), San Diego, CA.

Snee, R. D. (1995). *Listening to The Voice of The Employee.* Quality Progress, January, 1995, p. 91-95.

Steve, M. (1984). *Problem Solving and Decision Making: a Review of The Literature.* In A. H. Areson & J.J Decaro (Eds.), Learning and development: Volume 1, (pp. 319-369).

Struebing, L. (1995). *Is Performance Being Managed for The Long Term?.* Quality Progress, February, 1996, p. 14.

Struebing, L. (1995). *Report Finds That Managers Who Don't Share Power With Employees Lose Competitive Advantage.* Quality Progress, November, 1995, p. 16.

Taylor, W. L. & Cangemi, J. P. (1983). *Participative Management and The Scanlon Plan - a Perspective on its Philosophy and Psychology.* Psychology, A Quarterly Journal of Human Behavior, 20, No. 1, 42-46.

Tuttle, G. R. & Lester, R. I. (1993). *Employees Provide Supervisors With Feedback.* Quality Progress, November, 1993, p. 160.

U.S. General Accounting Office. (1988). *Employee Involvement. Issues for Agencies to Consider in Designing and Implementing Programs* (Report GAO/ggd-88-82). Washington, DC: U.S. General Accounting Office.

U.S. General Accounting Office. (1981). *Productivity Sharing Programs: Can They Contribute to Productivity Improvement?* U.S. General Accounting Office, Document Handling and Information Services Facility, Gaithersburg, MD.

Vough, C. F. & Asbell, B. (1975). *Tapping The Human Resource - a Strategy for Productivity.* New York: American Management Association.

Wheeless, T. A., Wheelas, L. R., & Howard, R. D. (1982). *An Analysis of The Contribution of Participative Decision- Making and Communication With Supervisors as Predictors of Job Satisfaction.* Paper presented at the Annual Forum of the Association for Institutional Research (22nd), Denver, CO.

Wongruangwisarn, P. (1980). *Managerial Leadership Style and Organization Effectiveness in Large Manufacturing Organizations in Bangkok.* Unpublished doctoral dissertation, University of Oklahoma, Norman, OK.

Zwerdling, D. (1980). *Workplace Democracy: a Guide to Workplace Ownership, Participation & Self-Management Experiments in The United States & Europe.* New York, NY: Harper Colophon Books.

Index

For Product Safety Concerns and Information please contact our EU
representative GPSR@taylorandfrancis.com
Taylor & Francis Verlag GmbH, Kaufingerstraße 24, 80331 München, Germany

www.ingramcontent.com/pod-product-compliance
Ingram Content Group UK Ltd.
Pitfield, Milton Keynes, MK11 3LW, UK
UKHW021822240425
457818UK00006B/41